TREKKING ACROSS AMERICA

Met these People on Desert

MRS. CHARLOTTE PALMER and sons, Ed and Ross, with their little dog, Zoe May, making an overland trip on foot, over the Lincoln Highway, from Omaha to Frisco.

1915

TREKKING ACROSS AMERICA

AN UP-CLOSE LOOK AT A
ONCE-POPULAR PASTIME

Lyell D. Henry Jr.

University of Iowa Press * Iowa City

University of Iowa Press, Iowa City 52242
Copyright © 2024 by Lyell D. Henry Jr.
uipress.uiowa.edu
Printed in the United States of America

Cover design by Brad Norr
Text design and typesetting by Sara T. Sauers
Printed on acid-free paper

Library of Congress Cataloging-in-Publication Data
Names: Henry, Lyell D., 1935– author.
Title: Trekking across America: An Up-Close Look at a
Once-Popular Pastime / Lyell D. Henry Jr.
Description: Iowa City: University of Iowa Press, [2024] |
Includes bibliographical references.
Identifiers: LCCN 2024003558 (print) |
    LCCN 2024003559 (ebook) |
    ISBN 9781609389796 (paperback; acid-free paper) |
    ISBN 9781609389802 (ebook)
Subjects: LCSH: Walking (Sports)—United States—History.
Classification: LCC GV1071 H46 2024 (print) |
    LCC GV1071 (ebook) |
    DDC 796.510973—dc23/eng/20240314
LC record available at https://lccn.loc.gov/2024003558
LC ebook record available at https://lccn.loc.gov/2024003559

CONTENTS

Preface

ABOUT THIRTY YEARS AGO, AS I WAS FLIPPING THROUGH THE WARES OF A dealer in vintage postcards, I came upon a card that had been incorrectly filed. It fell outside my collecting lines but was so instantly beguiling that I had to give it a closer look. That card showed two boys standing behind a cluster of roller skates of a very antiquated style. Wording across the top of the postcard claimed that the boys, Abe Levine and Max Brody, were roller-skating from New York to San Francisco! The inscription on their sweaters touted "Young's Skates New York," presumably the company that had provided their skates and perhaps even some financial support for their trip in return for the advertising. Bearing a May 25, 1910, postmark, the postcard had been sent by the two young skaters from Buffalo, New York, to a recipient in Vernon, New York, and conveyed a reassuring message: "Are OK, from the boys, Abe Levine & Max Brody."

What a charming item! It also prompted so many intriguing questions. Who were Abe and Max? Did Young's Skates put them up to this stunt? How did they skate on mud, which is what America's roads mostly were at that time? Did they get all the way to San Francisco? I bought the card, of course—it's included in chapter 1 along with Abe and Max's story—not yet fully aware that it had opened a new line of collecting interest. But soon I had uncovered postcards (and a few photographs, too) issued by other unusual cross-country travelers, and today I have about 400 of them (and some collectors have holdings ranging far beyond that number).

As these cards and photos document, from the opening of the last decade of the nineteenth century until the United States entered World War I, and then for another decade following the war's end, America's roads and railroad tracks were filled with characters traveling in attention-getting ways across large swaths of the United States, often aspiring, like Abe and Max, to go the entire distance between New York City and San Francisco. Although most of these cross-country travelers moved on foot, some—again, for instance, Abe and Max—employed novel variations on ordinary walking, some proceeded on bicycles or in other leg-powered vehicles, and some, including even a few who lacked the use of their legs, joined in the long-distance fun by relying on unusual animal-drawn conveyances. Oddbeat and even frivolous as these jaunts might have been, however, certainly none was easygoing. Herein, I identify all those making these challenging excursions as "trekkers," intending that that term be understood as congruent with the first meaning of "to trek" found in most dictionaries—for instance, "to make one's way arduously" (*Merriam-Webster*) or "to make a slow and arduous journey" (*American Heritage*).

But who were these people on the postcards? And what did their antics disclose about American life and culture in those years? Determining where and how to find the information I needed to answer those questions stumped me for many years.

What at last opened the way to learning more about this activity and its participants were the online newspaper archives that have become available in recent years. Because the trekkers were considered newsworthy—and also worked hard at self-promotion—reporters and editors took note of them, producing countless articles that can be tapped today, thanks to the possibility of identifying and retrieving them from the scanned newspapers in the archives. The newspaper accounts, I found, hold an enormous amount of information about the trekkers and their odysseys. The available early newspaper coverage even makes it possible in many instances to trace trip routes and—when coverage abruptly ceases—to know when and where particular journeys likely faltered and ended.

At first, I used my postcard holdings to cue my searches in the newspaper archives, but soon I was adept at digging up articles about many more eye-catching travelers than were depicted on those cards. Looking also for antecedents of this intriguing line of travel, I uncovered newspaper documentation of a handful of cross-country jaunts made on foot between 1867 and 1890. In sum, my initial idle wondering about these travelers ended at last in my assembling a great deal of information about many of them. And so delightful were their stories that I finally decided that they and the extraordinary activities in which they engaged merited a closer look and a wider sharing, and this book is the result.

Although I open each chapter with a brief discussion of some general features of the trekking phenomenon, most of the book's pages are given over to brief accounts of the trekkers and their journeys. Each vignette is accompanied by at least one image, usually a postcard or a photo but sometimes a newspaper illustration. Although I did not succeed in finding images of several of the trekkers I discuss, for several others I have included more than one image. Unless indicated otherwise, the postcards and photos are from my collection.

The characters in this book are, of course, only a portion of all the trekkers who were on the road; they are not even all of those for whom I could retrieve substantial coverage from the newspaper archives. But a selection was necessary, and my choices were governed not only by the need to identify and illustrate all principal features of this long-running field of activity but also by a determination that no case of great human interest or unusual zaniness be left out.

Soon after beginning my inquiry, I discovered that there were sometimes time gaps in the available newspaper coverage of specific treks and, even more frustrating, that available articles sometimes contained conflicting, dubious, or obviously erroneous information. Perhaps some of these problems can be attributed to lax standards of reporting, but more likely they can be traced to the trekkers' claims, which often smacked of tall tales and underwent changes in successive iterations. Although I proceeded cautiously through many hundreds of hefty newspaper files, I doubtless have incorporated errors into some of the vignettes I offer here. However, I'm confident that I've got the main lines of these stories right. To avoid cluttering my brief accounts, I have forgone the use of endnotes or listings of all the newspaper articles I consulted, but in many places in my text I do indicate sources and dates of directly quoted material. In my bibliographic essay, I also identify sources other than newspaper articles that I consulted while writing this book.

Because my focus in this book is on cross-country trekking as a component of American popular culture in the late nineteenth and early twentieth centuries, there are aspects of trekking that I don't address. Several of the figures I treat, for instance, are recognized today as pioneers of an activity called ultrawalking or ultrarunning, but readers will need to look to other sources (I cite one in my bibliographic essay) for coverage of those figures under that heading. My attention was also directed mainly to trekking done across the North American continent.

At that same time, trekking was also flourishing in Europe, but I'm not aware of any connections between the activities on the two sides of the Atlantic Ocean other than the fact that American trekkers claiming to do round-the-world treks sometimes got to Europe, while European trekkers engaging in world tours showed up in the United States more often. Also, with only two exceptions, none of the treks presented here occurred after 1930. Trekking across America continued thereafter, of course—in fact, right up to the present time—but the focus of this book is on the cross-country trekking that flourished during its heyday.

Several persons provided very valuable assistance to me as I worked on this book, and I want to acknowledge their help and extend my thanks to them. Holly Carver, former director of the University of Iowa Press, contributed good counsel both when I was still struggling to define this project and several times later when it was underway. Karen Copp, associate director and design and production manager at the University of Iowa Press, advised me on all matters concerning the reproduction of the images in this book. David Brenzel, former historian at the Marion Historical Society and Museum in Marion, Iowa, shared his holdings of nineteenth-century newspaper articles about cross-country trekkers as well as the letters that Seth Wilbur Payne sent to a New York newspaper during his trek. Russell Rein, fellow collector of odd stuff, supplied images of three postcards in his collection. Kenneth Wilson, author of an excellent book on early twentieth-century real-photo postcards, shared his expertise and let me use a rare item from his collection. Wayne Shannon, longtime friend and retired political science professor, confirmed the accuracy of some historical assertions that I make in chapter 3. Phil Brown, generous brother-in-law, secured at an obscenely high price in an eBay auction a very rare postcard for my use in this book. Peter Balestrieri, Special Collections librarian at the University of Iowa Libraries, made a valiant effort to locate a still elusive image for my use. And, certainly no less helpful than the foregoing persons, my wife, Gretchen Holt, kindly tolerated my many retreats to my desk during the years when my main attention was directed to writing this book.

Finally, deserving a special salute for his good help to me is Jim Hill, a gifted writer and editor and also my racquetball partner three times a week during the past fifteen years. As I worked my way through many drafts, Jim read all of them and provided invaluable critiques that led to my making many improvements. At our racquetball sessions, Jim was always ready to discuss book-related matters of concern to me during our breaks between the second and third games. In sum, Jim was of immense assistance to me in writing this book, and for that, for his friendship, and for his willingness to continue to play racquetball with me despite my fast-sinking skill in that department, I extend to him my most sincere thanks.

TREKKING ACROSS AMERICA

PROLOGUE

In Edward Payson Weston's Footsteps

MERICA'S FAVORITE PASTIME wasn't always baseball. For several decades in the latter half of the nineteenth century, that distinction was held by pedestrianism—that is, competitive walking. Although pedestrianism didn't make big strides in the United States until after the Civil War ended in 1865, it moved fast in the 1870s and early 1880s to become this country's hottest spectator sport, one that also attracted substantial amateur participation. Big-time competitive pedestrianism then began to wane later in the 1880s. By that time, however, it had already prepared the way for the flourishing of a new variant of pedestrianism, one that featured a multitude of fascinating characters crossing large parts of the country, mostly on foot but sometimes in even more conspicuous ways. This extravagant show, which I call the performance phase of pedestrianism, stayed strong for forty years.

In recent years, several excellent books have examined that original competitive phase of pedestrianism, recounting the sport's major participants and events and establishing its significance in the social history of the United States in the nineteenth century. In this book, I continue the story of pedestrianism by treating the performance phase that succeeded the competitive phase. In each of the chapters that follow, I comment briefly on aspects of this unusual activity but then turn quickly to sketching accounts of the actual participants and their performances. The seventy-six vignettes and accompanying images treat nearly one hundred of these eccentric expeditions and vividly depict a remarkable activity in the history of American popular culture.

Although these peripatetic performers are the subject of this book, a full accounting of them requires us first to know something about that original competitive phase of pedestrianism, a matter that I address in this prologue. As will soon be seen, an enterprising American played an outsize part in the flowering of both competitive and performance pedestrianism.

In the 1870s and early 1880s, when pedestrian competition was at high tide and pedestrian events attracted huge followings, newspapers throughout the country frequently marveled at the "walking fever" or "pedestrian mania" sweeping the United States, and sporting publications burgeoned with full coverage of pedestrian events. A leader among those publications was the *New York Clipper*, whose weekly coverage documented the advance of the sport. In the "Pedestrianism" section in its November 30, 1867, issue, for instance, the *Clipper*'s reportage of eleven pedestrian events taking place in the United States showcases nicely the scope and features of pedestrianism at that time. It also discloses the widespread enthusiasm pushing the sport's imminent emergence as a national favorite.

Four entries in that November 30 issue chronicled walk- or race-against-time events. In three of these, either concluded or forthcoming in New York, Wisconsin, and Kansas, a solitary contestant undertook to walk one hundred miles inside of twenty-four hours for prize money. Bookmakers offered odds on these events, of course, and the *Clipper* reported sad consequences for bettors who put their money on one failing contestant: "Many amateur sporting men lost heavily on him. One man, it is said, bet all his available cash, and a gold watch, in favor of Carlin, and of course lost." In the fourth walk against time noted in the column, an experienced walker proposed to walk from Chicago to New Orleans—about 1,500 miles—within twenty days in pursuit of a $2,000 stake. It was the judgment of the *Clipper*, however, that "tall walking will be required to accomplish the feat, and it is extremely doubtful if seventy miles a day can be averaged; nature will scarcely endure such a tax upon her powers as that."

Four more entries in that *Clipper* column described contests in which two men competed to win a cash prize for the best time achieved (both running and walking allowed) over a set course. Two of those accounts were especially striking. One announced an upcoming race over a three-mile course pitting Harding, an American, against De Kelso, a Canadian, for a $2,000 prize; to the winner would also go the (previously unheard of) title of "Champion of the United States and the New Dominion."

Vividly portrayed in another entry was a two-mile race that took place on Long Island between Ike Kemble and Jim Palmer for a $300 prize. As the *Clipper* reported, "at about half-past twelve o'clock the men appeared upon the ground, Ike being attired in a pink shirt, yellow tights and black patent leather belt, while Jim wore a scarlet shirt, tights of flesh color, and blue and white trunks." The race ended in a tie at nine minutes and thirteen seconds, however, necessitating the scheduling of a rematch.

Not only were pedestrian competitors already numerous, more were in the pipeline—or so one could conclude from a brief *Clipper* item headed "Juvenile Pedestrians": "On the 18th inst., fifteen lads set out on a pedestrian pilgrimage from Hartford, Ct., to Manchester and back, eighteen miles in all. Two of them did it in nine hours, the remainder failed. This is what we should call Westonianism down East."

"Westonianism"? What was that? No reader would have had any difficulty knowing that the term referred to the enormous impact on pedestrianism in the United States made by Edward Payson Weston, a young publisher and itinerant book salesman living in Providence, Rhode Island. Indeed, so prominent was Weston in this new line of sporting activity that he could fairly be tagged as the father of the pedestrian craze in America or, in the words of author John Cumming in his book *Runners and Walkers: A Nineteenth Century Sports Chronicle*, "the man who invented walking." The November 30 issue of the *Clipper* also provided a lengthy report about Weston's latest activity: walking from Portland, Maine, to Chicago.

Weston advanced to his leading place in pedestrianism quite by accident. His earliest recognition as a pedestrian came in 1861, when, having bet on Stephen Douglas in the 1860 presidential election, he was obliged, as the loser, to walk from Boston to Washington, D.C., to attend the inauguration of President Lincoln. (Taking ten days and four hours for the trip, he missed the presidential oath taking by four hours but did get to the inaugural ball and managed to shake Lincoln's hand.) His novel walk was a newsworthy sensation that brought him much gratifying attention, but soon enough he was back in the familiar routines of business and family life in Providence. Inclined throughout his entire adult life to live beyond his means, he already owed money to various creditors, and he proceeded to go deeper into debt. When a business acquaintance, George Goodwin, asked in 1867 whether he might be interested in taking on

The souvenir photos that Weston sold to adoring fans in 1867 present an image of a lean and resolute young man of twenty-eight years.

another long-distance walk, this time for a big potential payout, Weston was eager to hear the details.

Goodwin proposed the following. He would bet a fellow businessman $10,000 that Weston could walk from Portland to Chicago within thirty days. If he succeeded, Weston would get $4,000. If, during his walk, he could also cover one hundred miles within a twenty-four-hour period, he would receive another $6,000. Weston would have five opportunities during the trek to attempt this walk against time. Ignoring the protests of family members, he accepted the proposition, not yet knowing that he had thereby taken his first step into a new career as a professional pedestrian—a career line, moreover, of which he was the principal founder.

Weston took off from Portland on October 29, 1867, and when he arrived in Chicago twenty-six days later, on Thanksgiving Day, he had qualified for the $4,000 award. Both throughout his trek and upon his arrival, he was met by enthusiastic crowds; less gratifying were the rumors and newspaper accounts suggesting that the failure of each of his five tries to complete the assigned walk against time had something to do with accommodating the gambling interests of his sponsors. The *New York Clipper*, which followed his progress closely in successive issues, in its November 30 article acknowledged the huge crowds turning out to greet Weston but also pointed to some suspicious features of the failure of his third try at the hundred-mile test. Although the *Clipper* believed that Weston's handlers were the source of any skullduggery, charges made in other places clouded his reputation and achievement. Irksome, too, was press coverage that ignored the athletic aspects of his walk and treated him only as a mere showman engaging in a silly stunt.

Despite these questions about its legitimacy, respectability, and social value, Weston's Portland-to-Chicago trek quickly had some big effects, which were summarized nicely by the *Liberty (IN) Herald* on December 10, 1868: "The daily papers throughout the country have been teeming with Weston news and gossip ever since his departure from Portland, and as a consequence a great many attempts are being made by sportive young men to perform great pedestrian feats. In fact, walking is becoming a mania in different portions of the country." Weston, too, was soon engaged in more pedestrian events that lifted his renown, along with the public's newfound enthusiasm for these competitions, to even greater heights over the next few years.

By 1870, no one could doubt Weston's athletic prowess any longer. In that year, for instance, he completed the standard hundred-mile, twenty-four-hour challenge in less than twenty-two hours. By then, too, he was ready to abandon the kinds of events done mainly for the purposes of antic displays—for example, walking the final half hour backward in a ten-and-a-half-hour walk of fifty miles, a bit of cuteness he contracted to do on thirty occasions. Meanwhile, his increasing renown as a pedestrian prompted competitive challenges from others aspiring to cash in on the new endeavor. Eventually disdaining solitary performances carried out along railroad rights-of-way, on muddy country roads, or in roller-skating rinks in remote small towns, he began to concentrate instead on meeting topflight American and British competitors in races done indoors in large urban arenas, such as New York City's Madison Square Garden.

Those races, cheered on by thousands of raucous, booze-infused ticket buyers drawn from all social strata of American urban life, typically continued around the clock for six agonizing days and nights. During that time the contenders walked 500 miles or more, pushing on wearily through air filled with cigar smoke, crowd noise, and band music. The winners always got very large cash prizes and sometimes also a bejeweled championship belt, and for their part the fans could hope to tap their fair shares of the enormous amounts placed in wagers. These were the features of a golden age of competitive walking, during which Weston and other professional pedestrians ranked among the most celebrated athletes in the United States. When tobacco companies began in the 1880s to insert cards bearing images of famous sports figures into cigarette packs, pedestrians were among the first to be so honored, holding their own even against boxers and baseball players.

Staying strong throughout the 1870s, that golden age of pedestrian activity reached its zenith in the opening years of the 1880s. But then began the decline, and by the end of the decade the glory years of pedestrianism were over, and the sport was knocked from the top place in public favor by professional baseball as well as by newly emerging crazes for bicycling and roller skating. As big-time professional pedestrianism began to recede, however, a different kind of pedestrian activity became prominent, characterized by large numbers of colorful characters roaming the United States in attention-getting jaunts on foot between New York City and San Francisco or other pairs of widely separated cities. For

On the cover of its March 19, 1879, issue, *Puck* magazine spoofed the "walking mania" then sweeping the country.

THE GREAT INTERNATIONAL WALKING MATCH AT GILMORE'S GARDEN.—DRAWN BY IVAN PRANISHNIKOFF.—[SEE PAGE 247.]

Raucous crowds turned out for pedestrian competitions in big-city arenas, as illustrated in the March 29, 1879, issue of *Harper's Weekly*.

the decade of the 1890s, I have so far identified thirty-two such treks (or at least their announcements), and many more than that occurred in each of the three opening decades of the twentieth century.

These were not the first transcontinental treks on foot undertaken for unconventional reasons having no connection to the exploration or settlement of the West. In addition to Weston's Portland-to-Chicago walk, at least a dozen more walking trips across large portions of the United States had already been attempted or accomplished between 1867 and 1890. Nor were all of these early long-distance odysseys inspired by Weston; in fact, the first known walk from New York City to San Francisco, done by one Seth Wilbur Payne, happened at the same time as Weston's walk in 1867 (it was duly noted, of course, in that November 30 issue of the *New York Clipper*). However, neither Payne nor any of the other early transcontinental walkers ever acquired the renown or influence of Weston. When people thought of pedestrianism, they thought foremost of Weston. Because he remained for a long time the most famous pedestrian of that era, his example and activities continued inescapably to shape the character of pedestrianism as it evolved.

Weston's impact on the rise and course of American pedestrianism did not rest only on his having created the vogue for intercity walking, or on his being the man to beat in the high-stakes walking contests taking place in big-city arenas, or on his achieving some truly prodigious walking feats. In addition to reaching these heights of athletic accomplishment, he turned pedestrianism into a glamorous realm of show-biz performance. As early as his 1867 walk from Portland to Chicago, he saw that the activity had just as much potential as a field of entertainment as it did of athletic endeavor. A showman who loved the adulation of an audience, he played to his admiring crowds, often joking with them, singing, tooting on his cornet, or tossing his cane as he walked. Recognizing, too, the importance of dressing for the part, he very quickly cultivated the appearance of a dandy. Ruffled shirts, velvet breeches, sometimes a silk sash and a cape, and always a walking stick in hand—these became components of his trademark. In sum, Weston not only groomed the audience for the gaudy road shows to come in pedestrianism's subsequent days, he also created some of the standard features of those shows.

Weston was not directly involved in coddling into being this late-coming manifestation of Westonianism, however. After completing his Portland-to-Chicago walk in 1867, he did no more intercity walks of similar long distances for the next forty years. But then, in 1907, at the height of the craze for such walks—and long after his strongest competitive years were behind him and his renown was in decline—he repeated his sensational earlier walk. He followed that up with two more highly publicized journeys on foot—from New York City to San Francisco in 1909 in 105 days and from Los Angeles to New York in 1910 in 75 days. Finally, in 1913, at the age of seventy-four, he walked from New York City to Minneapolis in sixty days. These cross-country walks late in his career renewed his fame as a pedestrian and gave further impetus to the already surging craze for such walks. Soon thereafter, some of the latter-day transcontinental trekkers began to cite beating Weston's time as a reason for hitting the trail.

Edward Payson Weston

When Weston trekked from New York to San Francisco in 1909,
his postcards depicted a fit and trim man of seventy years.

As early as his Portland-to-Chicago trek, the business-savvy Weston had spotted the moneymaking potential of selling photographs of himself to his fans. Here, once again, he pointed the way for the hundreds of later cross-country trekkers who also helped finance their trips by peddling postcards bearing their images and claims. Usually the cards could be produced cheaply enough for trekkers to sell them at two or three for a quarter or ten cents each and still make a handsome profit. These postcards survive in large numbers today and provide good evidence of the range of participants in this latter phase of pedestrianism. They reveal that both men and women participated as solitary trekkers, as married couples, or in other small groups comprised usually of two or three persons of the same sex; among the trekkers, too, were even whole families—father, mother, and children. The cards also show that animals frequently were on these expeditions, either coming along as companions or pulling support vehicles.

The surviving postcards indicate that these offbeat travelers must have numbered at least in the many hundreds, and that total gets pushed even higher by evidence found in articles retrieved from newspaper archives. Together, the postcards and the newspaper articles pin down the heyday for these zany expeditions as the four decades between 1890 and 1930, particularly the briefer span of years ranging from the opening of the twentieth century to the time of America's entry into World War I.

In the 1880s, Weston and other very early cross-country hikers were joined by some brave souls attempting to make the long trip by bicycle. The earliest cyclists to have a go at the trip did so on cumbersome and dangerous high-wheelers, moving as best they could on railroad rights-of-way and America's poor facsimiles of roads. By the end of that decade, they could at least ride the new so-called safety bicycles that were equipped with pneumatic tires, but a jaunt by bicycle across the United States remained a huge challenge. The twentieth century brought the flowering of other conspicuous and challenging means for making that trip, such as riding astride a donkey or behind a goat team, piloting a sled outfitted with wheels and pulled by a team of wolves, negotiating the frequently muddy roads on roller skates, or walking barefoot, backward, or even on stilts.

The persons making these odd treks claimed a wide variety of reasons for doing so, and in the chapters that follow I present the evidence bearing that out. The clearest fact about these travelers, however, is that, no matter how much their stated reasons varied, at bottom all were performers seeking public notice by their treks. That was obviously so for those traveling by bizarre means or under unusual stipulated conditions, but the explanations and claims that all concocted for their treks showed that all were extremely attentive to publicity. Upon arriving in a town or city, for example, they frequently headed straight to the office of the local newspaper, hoping to get good coverage in the next issue. Often, too, these trekkers were performers in the more familiar sense of that word—that is, after making impromptu arrangements with local theater managers, some treated audiences to concerts, animal acts, or lectures giving highly embellished accounts of their travels. And when they left a town to go on to another, they could also be assured that they would not soon be forgotten, thanks to all the postcards they left behind.

Probably most of the people who encountered these travelers, including most who bought those postcards, were well aware of them as performers and recognized that their claims might not be true and certainly should not be taken at face value. But this skepticism still left room for enjoying their spiels, and certainly the travelers did provide much entertaining fare at a time when such options were limited in small towns. They could readily draw a crowd when word spread of their arrival, and on those occasions the ten cents spent on a postcard was a small price to pay for the entertainment value received.

Small-town editors throughout the United States tended toward a jaundiced judgment of the showy trekkers, however, often referring to them in their newspapers as freaks, cranks, or lunatics. Their newspaper accounts also often challenged the truth of the trekkers' claims (especially claims of large cash prizes) and accused them of attempting to freeload, avoid work, and obtain food and lodging by false pretenses. For some editors, these unwanted visitors to their towns were the latest embodiments of a tradition of on-the-road hustle already well wrought by the likes of itinerant peddlers of dubious land investment schemes, garishly illustrated Bible concordances, or snake oil.

That last characterization can't be pushed very far, however. For most participants, long-distance trekking was not a career choice or a business venture undertaken in the belief that it would be a good means of earning a living, at least for the long term. Few trekkers sold anything other than postcards, booklets, and souvenir trinkets. Only a minority, mostly persons physically disabled or down on their luck, seem to have taken to the road with the intention of trying to secure a long-term livelihood there. To these can be added some who became so hooked on the nomadic life despite its rigors and dismal income-generating prospects that they kept at it for many years, decades even. For most able-bodied persons, however, such a life, yielding only meager returns that came at an enormous cost in time, energy, and comfort, would surely have been an unappealing option.

In any event, for those having a yen to perform, an entire continent now beckoned as an inviting stage. Doubtless the number of cross-country treks rose as fast as it did partly because, increasingly, such treks *could* be done (or at least attempted). The Civil War had brought an end to any hazards that might derive from sectional strife, the frontier was closing, and the "wild West" was rapidly ceasing to be very wild; indeed, the West was soon "won," and hostile encounters were no longer likely—although some then walking through the West did have unpleasant scrapes with tramps. Because the West was increasingly dotted with cities, towns, farms, and ranches, those traveling in novel ways were seldom very far from the populated clusters that they counted on to support their long journeys.

The advance of railroad tracks west of the Missouri River after 1869 also enabled the growth of long-distance trekking at that same time. Confronting the absence of decent roads in the United States, the early trekkers usually stuck to railroad rights-of-way. By doing so, they could avoid getting lost, follow a path relatively free from encumbrances or mud, and be assured of finding human contact, water, and shelter at the railroads' utility stations. However, the spacing of railroad ties did not make it easy to walk, bike, or push carts, which meant that the long-distance trekkers began to abandon the railroad tracks as soon as highways started to improve in the 1910s and 1920s. The improved roads also stimulated trekkers to attempt bizarre new crossings by motorized vehicles of idiosyncratic design, size, or adornment.

Automobiles had already begun to be recognized as a threat to pedestrians early in the twentieth century. Certainly, Weston learned about their dangers during his walk from Los Angeles to New York in 1910. On that trip, according to *A Man in a Hurry: The Extraordinary Life and Times of Edward Payson Weston* by Nick Harris, Helen Harris, and Paul Marshall, "Weston was increasingly unnerved and exasperated by sharing the road with cars. In a couple of places, drivers had hurried up behind him, then sounded their horn, making him jump with fright." Later during that same walk, his ankle was injured and he was almost rendered unconscious when a passing automobile grazed another walker and sent him hurtling into Weston. "This was not the last time Weston would be hurt by a car," his biographers record, but without providing details.

By the end of that decade, however, Weston had come safely to the end of his walking career, having completed 90,000 miles (by his estimate) on foot during his lifetime and finding himself still in good physical and mental condition. In March of 1927, however, one week after his eighty-eighth birthday, he was struck by a taxicab in New York City and so seriously injured that he was confined to a wheelchair thereafter and became bedridden a year later. After one more year, he died in 1929 at the age of ninety. His passing coincided with the ending of the pedestrian phenomenon in whose development he had played such a dominant part, and in both instances the principal cause was that looming new adversary of pedestrians and pedestrianism: the motor vehicle.

In the pages ahead, I bring back to life some of the many characters who once followed in Weston's footsteps and roamed the United States during pedestrianism's performance phase. Although all of the chapters open with a brief general discussion of some feature of the long-distance walking craze, most of the pages are given over to specific trekkers. The trekkers I highlight are, of course, only a fraction of those who were on the road, but I have selected them to illustrate the full range of this phenomenon, including the types of persons participating in it and their modes of trekking, their claimed reasons for taking to the road, and their specific performances. In my epilogue, I present some final musings about these offbeat crossings and their place in American popular culture and history.

CHAPTER 1

Why Trek? Wagers and Prizes

WHY WOULD ANYONE CHOOSE to take on all the discomforts involved in walking several thousand miles across the North American continent? Those brave or crazy enough to attempt these treks gave various reasons for doing so (very often, more than one reason), but probably the motivating factor cited most often was a substantial sum of money allegedly available as a prize or payoff of a wager upon successful completion of the trek. Perhaps Weston's well-publicized big-money walk in 1867 had something to do with the fact that such treks caught on so quickly. Of a known dozen or so treks attempted before 1890, at least eight were walks on a wager. After 1890, cross-country treks purportedly done for money or other prizes came on in great profusion. These cash prizes may often seem implausibly meager in relation to the amount of time and effort invested. However, consider that according to a well-accepted method of calculation, $1,000 in 1896 was the equivalent of a hefty $37,889 today, and in 1908 it was still worth $34,876 in today's terms.

Treks allegedly having cash payouts had some standard features or requirements. For one thing, anyone putting up money for a prize or placing money at risk on a wager was likely to specify some stiff conditions. Almost always, of course, there would be time limits and a ban on doing any part of the journey by any means other than walking, but further requirements could make the trek even more difficult (and even more newsworthy). For example, some trekkers had to begin the trek wearing a newspaper suit that could be replaced by conventional clothing only as the trekker acquired the needed money by working or receiving donations along the way; some had to start the trek with no money but return with a specified sum acquired by any legal means;

and some had to meet a woman along the way and marry her before completing the trek.

Then there was the problem of verifying compliance with the terms of the contest or wager. In a trek ranging over thousands of miles, most of it done out of sight of the sponsoring parties, the many opportunities to cheat could amply feed any inclinations to do so. Elaborate—and expensive—arrangements might therefore be specified to ensure compliance; on his 1867 trek from Portland to Chicago, for example, Weston was accompanied all the way by four "trustworthy and reliable men" (presumably following him on horseback or by carriage). Each side of the high-stakes wager had chosen two of these gentlemen, and all were there to make sure that nothing untoward occurred and the terms of the wager were met. Many of the other pre-1890 wager-walkers were also accompanied on their treks by similar guarantors of their honesty.

But how often were such elaborate and costly arrangements likely to be made merely to facilitate a trek? For that matter, wasn't a high-stakes trekking challenge itself likely to be an exceedingly rare event? Surely, few big-time gamblers would want to risk money on contests taking so long to complete, so open to the possibility of cheating, and requiring such expensive oversight. Big-city newspapers, sporting publications, and some businesses (for instance, shoe-manufacturing companies) might occasionally put money into supporting trekkers for their own advertising purposes, and sometimes, too, fraternal lodge brothers or other small groups of friends might pass the hat to raise a sum with which to challenge a buddy's boasts. Otherwise, couldn't one reasonably conclude that not many persons, publications, or organizations, even those flush with cash, would be ready to fritter away large chunks of money on activities so trivial or requiring so much careful arranging and monitoring? As solid as that line of thought may seem, however, it appears to be countered by the mounting numbers of trekkers after 1890 who claimed to be walking for big stakes posted by just such big-money sources.

Unlike Weston and the other earliest wager-walkers, most trekkers after 1890 were not accompanied by one or more persons there to guarantee compliance with the wagers' terms. Instead, wager-walkers now usually carried logbooks in which they secured the postal cancellations or signatures of mayors or other officials of the cities and towns visited on their prescribed routes. This practice not only fell short of guaranteeing fidelity to all the wagers' terms, however; it also buttressed the conviction that cross-country trekkers were nuisances and did nothing to stifle rising doubts about whether those wagers were real. In fact, newspaper editors began very early to reject as bogus most claims presented by the wager-walkers, especially their accounts of rich but anonymous benefactors who seemed so preposterously eager to post large sums in order to encourage and reward their efforts.

In one oft cited version of the story, the benefactor was a "wealthy New York clubman" whose existence the *Waterloo (IA) Times-Tribune* derided in an article published on July 12, 1912, under this headline: "Mysterious Angel Makes Many Bets / Freaks Circle the Globe at Instance of Strange Philanthropist / In an Endless Chain / Is Willing to Give Up $25,000 Just to Have Them Do It." Editors also treated as a tall tale another frequent account in which wealthy idlers lounging at their big-city club fall into an argument about whether a particular long-distance walk could be completed under certain restrictions, whereupon they enter into a big-money bet and hire someone to give the trek a try. Scoffing newspaper stories sometimes pointed out, too, the curious and telling fact that rarely, if ever, did one hear of a highly touted wager being won or paid.

Not only their colorful stories but the wager-walkers themselves were often handled roughly in American newspapers. Editors delighted, for instance, in publishing reports that the latest visiting trekker was allegedly spotted sneaking out of town at night by freight train—in other words, was a fraud. In addition to facing the usual ridicule heaped on trekkers as freaks and lunatics, wager-walkers were often denounced in the newspapers as pests, "peripatetic nuisances," and (nastiest label of all) tramps. By tramps were meant, of course, persons having no visible means of support who chose not to work but instead traveled from place to place seeking handouts. For sure, that description seemed to fit nicely the many trekkers who claimed that their wager agreements required them not to purchase or work for food and lodging but instead to rely entirely on the kindness of strangers for all necessities.

A writer in the *Biloxi (MS) Daily Herald* on January 15, 1904, argued that those purporting to walk on wagers had, in fact, brought new vigor to an old racket. "The tramp is started on a new process of unfolding," the reporter alleged. "What seemed a dull shell, hiding only the spent fires of a congenitally feeble character, is budding. The tramp is now appealing to the strongest sentiment in the human heart, the sporting instinct. He comes to us with the declaration that he is traveling on a wager." So efficacious was this new tactic in serving the cause of freeloading, the writer continued, that "if the tramps are clever enough, their hardships may soon cease. They may all be walking on wagers."

Joining in the chorus denunciating wager-walkers, the *Hershey (PA) Press* in its January 9, 1913, issue called them out for exploiting "a cheap way of getting into the lime-light and pandering to the itch for notoriety that is becoming so common." The article concluded with a sentiment widely expressed in American newspapers at that time: "Working for wages, we think, is better than walking for wagers, and is it not about time the public had a rest?"

That longed-for rest from the siege of wager-walkers didn't begin to happen until the time of America's entry into World War I. By then, this species of trekker had been wandering America for fifty years, and their numbers ran well into the hundreds. Although most will doubtless remain unrecognized forever, surviving postcards and newspaper articles make it possible to know something about some of them. The following samples illustrate the wide array of these trekkers and the wagers into which they claimed to have entered.

The Wheelbarrow Man

In 1878, R. Lyman Potter was a thirty-seven-year-old upholsterer and widower living with his two young children in Albany; in that year, he also walked from that city to San Francisco—perhaps the first trekker known to have gone coast to coast on a wager. On May 22, when a reporter for the *Fort Wayne (IN) Weekly Sentinel* asked him how that had come about, Potter explained, "Waal, it all came from too d——n much talk. We [that is, a group of mechanics] wuz talkin' about work and earnin' money, and hard times, etc., and I said I'd wheel a wheelbarrow to San Francisco for a dollar a day rather'n be without work. The Albany fellows took me up and made up $1,000, which is now on deposit in Albany. I had nothin' to do and as I wouldn't back down, I started out and here I am."

Many newspapers quickly took note of Potter, usually treating him derisively as a lunatic or a fool, and certainly his appearance suggested something out of the ordinary. Upset by the reelection of President Grant in 1872, Potter vowed not to trim his beard again until a Democrat was elected president. Sporting shaggy black whiskers untrimmed for over five years and pushing a homemade wooden wheelbarrow, he was soon widely known as the Wheelbarrow Man, and his arrival was eagerly awaited in the towns and cities on his route.

To win the $1,000, Potter needed to push his wheelbarrow for 4,085 miles from Albany to San Francisco within 215 walking days, Sundays excluded (250 total days including Sundays). Accompanied by a watcher (the first of several on the journey) to prevent cheating, he set out on April 10, 1878. After seven days, he had gone 125 miles, only modestly exceeding his needed minimum rate of 19 miles per walking day. Rain, blisters, and sore muscles had made those days so unpleasant that he considered quitting. The newspapers had predicted his failure, however, so he was determined to keep going. Across New York he used old turn-pike roads, but thereafter he mostly followed railroad tracks.

Potter started with only $3.55, expecting he would get more money as needed by working. That never happened, however, and several times he had to wire home for money. He calculated his total out-of-pocket expenses for the trek as $400, but some of that total was offset by money received for carrying letters to San Francisco and posting advertisements

Lyman Potter's souvenir photo gives full display
to both his whiskers and his wheelbarrow.

on his wheelbarrow. Only rarely, too, did he need to pay for meals and sleeping accommodations.

On October 5, several hundred persons welcomed Potter as he arrived at Sacramento. He had averaged twenty-seven miles per walking day for the trek and was within easy reach of its end in San Francisco by the December 15 deadline. As he approached that city on October 27, he was met by a marching band that escorted him to a large amusement facility, Woodward's Gardens, where an estimated 15,000 persons cheered his arrival. For several weeks he remained there, basking in adulation and earning money by lecturing and demonstrating his walking as he completed on-site the final 90 miles of the trek's required 4,085 miles.

The hoopla soon brought on a challenge from one Leon Peter Federmeyer (more about him shortly) to compete in pushing wheelbarrows back to New York for a $1,500 prize posted by some "gentlemen of means" in San Francisco. Potter accepted, and the contestants left on December 8, 1878. When Federmeyer arrived in New York seven and a half months later, however, Potter was only in Illinois and, in fact, didn't reach New York until the end of 1881—that is, three years after beginning the return trip. Clearly, Potter had become hooked on trekking and had found numerous ways to cash in on it, such as selling his photo, lecturing, giving demonstrations, and performing in theaters with a "singing" pet wolf. His mileage rate unavoidably fell, too, as he filled his wheelbarrow with mineral and animal specimens and Indian relics, eventually bringing its weight to a hefty 240 pounds.

Finally reaching home in Albany early in 1882, Potter married but was off again at year's end on a wager-walk to New Orleans. Finding that this one didn't go well, however, in Tennessee he decided to return home. He never got there but was hit by a train and killed in North Carolina. His pet singing wolf was found close by. The sole reported comments by Potter's widow were that she would donate the wolf to a menagerie and hoped she could get $1,000 from the sale of the wheelbarrow.

Wheelbarrow Rivalry

Lyman Potter and Leon Peter Federmeyer began their entwined journeys from San Francisco to New York in 1878 just as winter was setting in, which would seem to confirm the view of most newspaper editors then that all transcontinental trekkers were lunatics. Knowing that they faced great risks, the trekkers agreed to travel together across the Sierra Nevadas. That portion of the trip did indeed prove to be daunting, featuring severe storms, much deep snow, and subzero temperatures. However, on Christmas Day, the intrepid duo reached Reno, and by mid-January they were at Battle Mountain, Nevada, where they parted ways. Federmeyer quickly pulled far ahead of Potter.

As his lead steadily grew, Federmeyer became the focus of the public's growing interest in this race, soon displacing Potter as the one referred to simply as the Wheelbarrow Man. Dressed distinctively in a red flannel shirt and black pantaloons and wearing a broad-brimmed straw hat, he was eagerly awaited and favorably received by communities along his entire route. In April, near Ellis, Kansas, Federmeyer and his wheelbarrow fell a full fifteen feet from a bridge. Although stunned and temporarily unresponsive, the next day he was on his way east again, and on July 24 he was in New York City.

Much of the public's fascination with Federmeyer derived from his backstory, which, culled from newspaper accounts, includes the following. Born in France in 1838, he fought and was wounded in the Franco-Prussian War. His profession was that of a "worker in hair," which meant in his case a women's hairdresser but also an artist whose medium was human hair. After his wife died, sometime in the early 1870s, he spent the next seven grief-filled years re-creating her image from strands of her hair. That close work put a great strain on his eyesight. Immigrating to the United States in 1876, he first worked as a hairdresser in New York City, where he also met William Moutoux, the world's most esteemed artist in hair, and continued to make pictures of his own in this unusual medium. A large landscape by Federmeyer won a silver medal at the Paris Exposition in 1878. However, the toll on his eyesight finally forced him to give up this kind of art. Thus, in 1878, according to an article published in the *Cincinnati Gazette* on May 27, 1879, "he accepted the

Leon Peter Federmeyer put his wheelbarrow front and center in his souvenir photo.

challenge to walk across the continent for want of something else to do which would not involve a strain upon his eyes."

Upon his arrival in New York City in late July, Federmeyer began at once to cash in on his new celebrity. In a six-day wheelbarrow-pushing contest held in a New York venue in August, he reached 407 miles and won a cash prize. On August 20, the *Los Angeles Herald* reported that some "gentlemen of means" opened discussions with him about exhibiting his wheelbarrow-pushing prowess in various cities on the East Coast, also noting that Federmeyer's "enthusiasm about wheelbarrow driving amounts to a passion." That passion soon propelled him to the pinnacle of walking performance: the six-day Astley Belt competition held in Madison Square Garden in September. Competing against Edward Payson Weston and other top professionals in this most prestigious of pedestrian events, Federmeyer placed tenth out of thirteen contestants, according to the *San Francisco Chronicle* on October 11, 1879.

Federmeyer's eyesight must have taken a big turn for the better, because in 1880 he won a silver medal in a San Francisco art competition for a portrait in hair of President-elect James Garfield. By the next year, he had a business there making portraits in hair and giving lessons in that arcane art. Still doing some wheelbarrow walking in 1881, he won a six-day event held in San Francisco against two others (one a woman), and in 1883 he began a much-ballyhooed wheelbarrow-pushing transcontinental race (neither contestant seems to have gotten past Denver, however). Thereafter, Federmeyer gave his attention mainly to hair work, still producing pictures (one of Victor Hugo was particularly admired) but increasingly developing new hairstyles. By 1890, he had relocated to Chicago, where he operated a hairstyling studio and, with a partner, also opened this country's first academy of hairstyling.

Federmeyer belonged to the faith-healing religious sect famous for Flat Earth advocacy that was led by Wilbur Glenn Voliva and ensconced in Zion City, Illinois. Believing prayer had cured him of a rupture, he became an increasingly zealous and active sect member. He died at the age of seventy-four after engaging in fervent prayer and testimony in an all-night service held on New Year's Eve, 1913.

The Poetical Pedestrian

Potter and Federmeyer likely were the earliest to walk across the United States on a wager, but they were not the first to spot the moneymaking potential of doing so. Excited by Weston's celebrated 1867 trek, in 1868 Mark Grayson, a down-at-the-heels actor, walked from Richmond, Virginia, to Omaha, giving sixty speeches on the way promoting the Democratic Party's presidential ticket of Horatio Seymour and Francis Preston Blair. Fired up by this experience, he concocted big plans for a transcontinental walk and, later, plans for a round-the-world walk. He evidently found no backers, however, because neither trek ever happened.

Dennis Collins, a California farmer, did complete a cross-country wager-walk in 1879. Of that early trek, the *Des Moines Register* on July 26, 1879, wrote this: "It appears a dispute arose in San Francisco between several gentlemen on the merits of the walk of Potter, the wheelbarrow man, when Mr. Collins, with an enthusiastic faith in his countrymen's ability to accomplish anything, declared himself willing to wager plenty of Irishmen could be found to beat Potter's time. A bet of $1,500 was made, and Mr. Collins himself . . . undertook to perform the task." Then, in 1884, J. S. Herriman, a professional pedestrian, claimed to have walked from California to New York in 118 days for a $5,000 prize. In that same year, Adrian Hitt, hailed as the Poetical Pedestrian, also walked on a wager from New York to San Francisco and then walked back on another wager. Like Dennis Collins but unlike most other wager-walkers, Hitt put his own money at stake in those walks.

Thirty-two years old in 1884, Hitt seems to have had no definite occupation, but he claimed to be an inventor and did, in fact, hold several patents. He appears also to have never resided in one state or region for long, but he did own a forty-acre farm in Missouri, even though he didn't work it or live there. Cranking out doggerel copiously, he bundled it for sale in pamphlets and books, one of which was somewhat immodestly titled *The New Shakespeare*. Hitt tapped into all these aspects of his life to meet the terms of a wager that resulted from an argument among friends about human endurance under sustained stress. Accepting a challenge to make a transcontinental trek within one hundred days for a prize of $2,000, he staked his farm and a half interest in one of his patents.

Not permitted by the agreement to take money on the trek, Hitt

That Adrian Hitt dressed like a baseball player is supported by this sketch from the *Police Gazette* of July 12, 1884.

planned to meet expenses by selling copies of four pamphlets of poems he wrote for the occasion. Pushing these in a wheelbarrow, he claimed to have sold 2,000 on the round trip. He also selected a costume for the trek consisting of a long-sleeved shirt, knee pants, and a white cap inscribed "New York to San Francisco." One newspaper article noted correctly that he looked like a baseball player.

Ninety-eight days after leaving New York City on June 19, 1884, Hitt was in San Francisco on September 24, ready to claim the $2,000 stake. The losing bettor now proposed a new two-for-one bet: Hitt's farm, patent, and $2,000 against $8,000 that Hitt couldn't make the return trek within ninety days. Hitt accepted, rested for several weeks, and took off on October 16. Eighty-nine days later he was in New York City, again winning the wager. Hoping to cash in on his success, he proposed to walk to the North Pole for a purse of $8,500 but had no takers, and so ended his walking career.

Hitt planned to use his winnings "to set up an inventors' shop . . . to take inventions that ain't quite invented yet and finish inventing them," according to the *Macon (GA) Weekly Telegraph and Messenger* of January 23, 1885. That likely didn't happen, but he did procure several more patents and pursued the development of an elevated "electrical railroad" that would go between Indianapolis and New York in four hours. He also claimed to have developed a novel method for reaching the North Pole, and to raise funds to carry this out he wrote his major poetical work, *The Grant Poem*, a biography of Ulysses Grant in 370 pages of rhymed couplets. On the final page, Hitt also settled a score with the many who had mocked his verse:

> May howling critics here abuse,
> Let each line, their silly mind peruse.
> Ah! critics! critics, may they be damned,
> Head first into Hades jammed!
> Critics? Ah! What love and justice,
> The damnedest fiends that ever cussed us!
> Such fiends should have no tongues to wag,
> Hellwards a fellow man to drag.

The Queen of Ties

Transcontinental trekking was inherently a performance activity having attention-getting and even some remunerative potential. No surprise, then, that two itinerant actors, both facing uncertain prospects for employment, sensed trekking's allure. As already noted, Mark Grayson pursued several trekking schemes, but none panned out. Zoe Gayton, a well-known actor in the 1870s and 1880s, fared much better; her 1890–91 wager-walk brought her big winnings, opened a new realm of performance for her, and gave her standing as the first woman to complete a transcontinental trek.

Zorika Gaytoni Lopez Ares was born in Madrid, Spain, in 1854; four years later, she came to New York City with her family. Her name became Zoe Gayton when she began her acting career at the age of fourteen. During the next twenty years, she went through several marriages, founded her own acting company, and performed in a full repertoire of plays presented throughout the United States and Europe. She was best known for her equestrian performances in *Mazeppa, or the Wild Horse of Tartary*, a four-act play based on a poem by Lord Byron. Taking the lead role, in the play's most thrilling scene Gayton was strapped to the side of a horse that then ascended on a special track almost to the stage's ceiling. Hard times came her way, however, when the bankruptcy of her company in 1885 was followed by its demise in 1889. She was out of work and stranded in San Francisco when the opportunity to take up transcontinental trekking opened in 1890.

Two different accounts of how Gayton came to her trek appeared in newspapers. One version had her bewailing her sad circumstances in a conversation with friends and exclaiming, "I know if I only had $2,000 to get a start with, I could make fame and fortune." When a listener offered to pay her that amount and her expenses if she would walk from San Francisco to New York, she accepted and was on her way the next day. A more likely account, however, had Gayton and other guests at a dinner party listening to George H. Clarke, a well-known "sporting man," speak admiringly of the achievement of two young men who had just ridden horseback from New York to San Francisco, averaging fifteen miles a day. When Gayton piped up to say that she, too, could make that rate walking, Clarke replied, "I'll wager $2,000 that you cannot do it."

ZOE GAYTON AND HER DOG.

Rejecting bloomers, Zoe Gayton trekked in a long woolen dress,
as depicted in the *New York Weekly Press* on March 25, 1891.

Gayton accepted the challenge, and within minutes others pushed the wager to $24,000, of which Gayton stood to get $12,000 if she did the trek within 225 days—that is, at an average of at least fifteen miles a day, as reported in the *Boston Daily Globe* of March 28, 1891.

Gayton left on August 27, 1890, accompanied by two pet cocker spaniels (one died on the trip), her theatrical manager, and a watcher to prevent cheating. Wearing bloomers at the start, she soon switched to long woolen dresses. Because the party stayed on train tracks most of the way, she was a familiar sight to railroad workers, who dubbed her the Queen of Ties. Until they reached the Midwest, the trekkers usually camped out at night, and for four days while crossing the Sierra Nevadas they had nothing to eat except game shot by the two men. They suffered often from cold weather; in September, Gayton sprained her ankle, delaying the trek for a week; and once, meeting an oncoming train, she jumped fourteen feet from a trestle but landed uninjured in mud. When the party at last reached New York City on March 28, thirteen days ahead of their deadline, Gayton's feet and legs were swollen, doctors declared her suffering from "nervous prostration," and she swore never to do such a walk again.

Flush with cash, Gayton reactivated her theatrical company, but within a year it had failed again. Setting aside her vow, she returned to trekking, beginning in 1892 with a $20,000 transcontinental walk routed by way of New Orleans. She appears to have pulled out in Texas, however, and failed to finish at least three other announced long-distance walks, including one around the world, during the next three years. Several shorter walks done in 1896 were her last activities, pedestrian or theatrical, to be recorded in newspapers. She died penniless and forgotten in Omaha in 1907 at the age of fifty-three, her obituary identifying an incurable nervous disorder as the cause. This time it wasn't trekking that set off the disorder but, rather, the loss of all her property the year before in the San Francisco earthquake. "Her closing days were the most trying of her career," read the obituary. Because her last husband (then deceased) had been a Mason, she at least got a dignified send-off provided by the Omaha lodge.

Police Gazette *Contenders*

An indication of a changing popular culture in the United States in the late nineteenth century was the rise of the *National Police Gazette*, the first mass-circulation magazine to offer an amalgam of lurid articles and pictures, ample sports coverage, and cheesecake (such as it was then). Under the creative leadership of its owner and editor, Richard K. Fox, the New York City–based *Police Gazette* catered to the tastes and interests of males who did their reading mostly in barbershops. Among Fox's many innovations was the promoting of competitive activities never heard of before, such as going the longest time without sleep, lifting the heaviest weight held by straps clenched between the teeth, and jumping from the highest bridge into the river below. In addition to chronicling these novel events in words and illustrations, Fox awarded gaudy *Police Gazette* medals to many of the winners—for instance, to a meat cutter for his performance in a butchering competition, a champion female weight lifter, a one-legged clog dancer, and the winning dog in a canine rat-killing contest held in a special arena set up by the magazine.

Transcontinental trekking and trekkers soon caught Fox's eye, of course. In the 1880s, the *Police Gazette*'s pages—printed on pink-tinted paper!—carried images and accounts of some of the trekkers and their efforts—for example, Adrian Hitt and his walk in 1884. In the next decade, however, Fox made bigger moves to cash in on the growing craze. When Zoe Gayton arrived in New York on her long walk in 1891, for instance, he tapped into her celebrity by whisking her away to a reception held in the *Police Gazette*'s editorial chambers. Throughout that decade, the *Police Gazette* also tantalized trekkers with the prospect of winning a bejeweled championship belt and engaged many of them in long-distance wager-walks for big stakes put up by the magazine.

Many of the events sponsored by the *Police Gazette* were walks between New York and San Francisco that had specified time limits and payouts of several thousand dollars, but several revealed Fox's continuing yen for more flamboyant and Barnumesque options. An early trekker to wear the black sweater bearing the magazine's name was a diminutive man named Frank Dram, who had no trekking background but whom Fox doubtless took on because he looked, in the words of a reporter for the May 14, 1891, edition of the *Dunkirk (NY) Evening Observer*, "like an

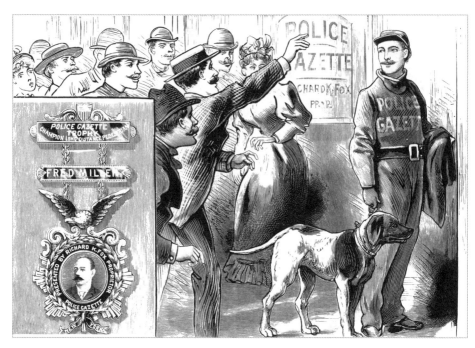

END OF A LONG TRAMP.

In its July 27, 1895, issue, the *Police Gazette* hailed Fred Miller and dog, Guess, upon their completion of a walk from New York to Jacksonville and back.

escaped dime museum freak." Fox then promoted with much hoopla in 1893 a $25,000 competition in which trekkers sponsored respectively by the *San Francisco Chronicle* and the *Police Gazette* walked in opposite directions between New York and San Francisco. And in 1895, when Fox learned of a Wisconsin man's plan to walk on stilts from Green Bay to New Orleans, he brought the event under the auspices of the *Police Gazette* at the very small cost of a $250 prize posted for the contender (who got no farther than Centralia, Illinois).

Fox often imposed a condition of strict poverty on the trekkers he sponsored—that is, they were not permitted to carry money or to otherwise secure food or shelter by begging or working but instead had to rely on the charity of the people they met along the way. This added show-biz color and drama to the treks but also increased their difficulty. Indeed, here may be the explanation of a curious fact about these treks:

although most were done by experienced walkers, many seem not to have been completed. Striking exceptions, however, were those done by Fred Miller, seemingly Fox's favorite pedestrian.

Miller came to public notice in 1893 when, accompanied by his pointer dog Guess, he completed a $2,000 wager-walk from San Francisco to New York (the *Police Gazette* might have been the sponsor). Like Frank Dram, Miller was very small—"a little, wiry fellow," one reporter wrote— which likely added to Fox's desire to have him wear the *Police Gazette* sweater on more walks. Fox enlisted Miller and Guess for a walk in 1894 from New York to New Orleans and back and then for another one the next year from New York to Jacksonville, Florida, and back. Bestowing a gold championship medal on Miller, Fox then engaged him for two more successful round-trip walks from New York; to Denver in 1896 and to El Paso in 1897. On these treks, Miller was permitted to earn his way by selling photos.

Miller then disappeared from public notice for seventeen years. When found by a reporter in 1914, he was still walking—seven miles a day as a letter carrier in Hammond, Louisiana. Citing his *Police Gazette* medal as evidence, he claimed still to be the "champion long-distance walker of the world."

A Strong Woman's Sad Story

At life's darkest hour, opportunity still may knock—so Helga Estby learned in 1896. The thirty-eight-year-old Helga and her husband, Ole, both immigrants from Norway, lived with their eight children on a farm near Spokane, Washington. Although the nation was finally recovering from the Panic of 1893, the Estbys' situation was bad. Serious injuries prevented Ole from working, and if taxes and the mortgage were not paid soon, they would lose the farm. But then a "friend in the East" chanced to put Helga in touch with a "wealthy woman in New York," who made an astonishing proposal.

Helga never knew who that rich New Yorker was, only that she had "invented a new style garment" for women and wanted to advertise its availability. Like the shorter skirts that were just then being introduced for bicycling, this new dress would give its wearers enhanced freedom of movement. How better to advertise it than to have it worn by two women walking across the country? The New Yorker proposed that Helga and her oldest child, Clara, age eighteen, be those women and that the matter be set up as a wager-walk for a prize of $10,000. Seeing the offer as a godsend, Helga got Clara's assent and, defying Ole's faint protests and the more vigorous ones arising from her other children and friends in their Scandinavian community, she signed on to do it.

The contract specified that, to qualify for the $10,000 payout, Helga and Clara would walk from Spokane to New York within seven months. They would meet and get the signatures of governors and mayors in all state capitals and other principal cities on the way. They would each start the trip with $5 and get more money only by working and selling photographs as they went. They would not beg. Upon reaching Salt Lake City, they would wear only the new-style dresses for the rest of the trek.

Helga and Clara left on May 5, 1896, traveling lightly, taking such things as toiletries, writing materials, and revolvers but no blankets or change of clothes. Usually sticking to railroad tracks, they averaged twenty-seven miles per day on walking days, but many of their days were spent sightseeing or, more often, earning money by cooking, sewing, and housecleaning. On one occasion, lost in Colorado, they went three days and two nights without eating, and on eight nights they had to sleep under the stars. However, very often they did receive free meals and

MRS. S. ESBY AND HER DAUGHTER CLARA
Who have just completed a walk from Spokane, Wash., to New York.

Helga and Clara Estby wore the latest in trekking costumes, as shown in the *Philadelphia Inquirer* on December 24, 1896.

overnight accommodations. In the western states, mountain lions and rattlesnakes were a problem, but tramps were a problem everywhere; several times the women deterred them with cayenne pepper, and once Helga shot a tramp in the leg.

On November 29, the walkers were in Canton, Ohio, where they spent a delightful hour at midday chatting with President-elect and Mrs. William McKinley, but thereafter the pressure to get moving was intense. The seven months since their start would be up on December 5—only six days ahead—and they were still more than 400 miles from New York. Clearly, they could not finish in that time, but Helga was counting on invoking a contractual provision that would allow them to extend their deadline to accommodate the time lost due to Clara's sprained ankle in Colorado and sickness in Nebraska.

The local press gave admiring coverage to Helga and Clara upon their arrival in New York on December 23, but the *New York Herald* noted that the meaning of a contractual provision "will have to be settled before the travelers know whether they win or lose the wager." The answer came late the next day: claiming that the contract covered only time lost due to sickness but not to injury, the sponsor would not pay the wager or even provide money for the Estbys' train fares back to Spokane.

Christmas Day was a grim one for the Estby women, who began looking for work the next day. In mid-April, still lacking money to buy train tickets, Helga learned that her daughter Bertha had succumbed to diphtheria earlier that month. Now desperate to get home, she appealed unsuccessfully to several charities; at last, a railroad executive gave them tickets to Chicago. They then walked to Minneapolis, where they earned enough money to get home. There they faced the wrath of family members and learned that diphtheria had also taken son Johnnie; soon, too, came the loss of the farm.

Despite family hostility and her trek's sad features, in 1913 Helga began to write an account of it that eventually ran to several hundred pages. The passage of forty-five years had not dulled two daughters' anger at their mother, however; upon Helga's death in 1942, they burned her manuscript. Fortunately, Helga's trek has since been fully recounted by Linda Lawrence Hunt in *Bold Spirit*, a book tapped amply for this account.

Trekking on an Empty Purse

In the final decades of the nineteenth century, the world-circling exploits of George Francis Train and Nellie Bly (as well as those of the fictional Phileas Fogg) stimulated many more attempts at circumnavigations of the globe; here, according to the *South Australian Register* of May 25, 1898, was "the latest thing in American freakishness or enterprise." Sometimes, however, these expeditions aimed not at setting a new time record but rather at exhibiting new attention-getting features. In that line, Emil C. Pfeiffer, who traveled under the name Paul Jones, stood out.

Claiming to be an 1889 graduate of Harvard, Paul Jones was, according to numerous newspaper reports, a handsome, affable young man greatly gifted at smooth talk. Profoundly self-assured, he characterized

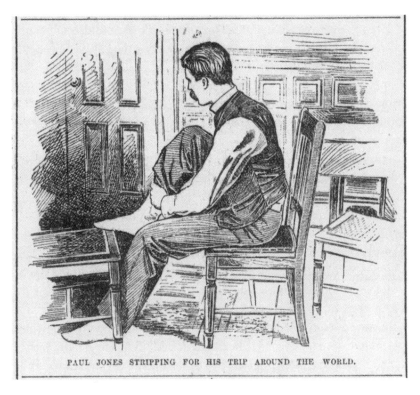

PAUL JONES STRIPPING FOR HIS TRIP AROUND THE WORLD.

In its issue of February 13, 1894, the *Boston Daily Globe* showed Paul Jones readying for his trek's start by undressing.

himself, as reported in the *Jersey City News* on May 14, 1894, as "one of those great American cranks who can do anything except earn his living by work." In keeping with that self-assessment, Jones made a $5,000 wager with some fellow members of the Boston Athletic Club: starting with neither money nor clothing, he would journey around the world in one year and return with $5,000. Many newspapers soon recounted admiringly how, in only two days' time, Jones had managed to go from a condition of penniless total nudity to having a full suit of clothes and more than $100 in his pocket.

Despite his spectacular start, Jones probably didn't complete the journey (in fact, he likely never even left the United States), and he was soon forgotten. However, some of his innovative methods for drawing attention were adopted by other long-distance walkers, one of whom was George Melville Boynton, a man as talented as Jones at putting on a good show.

Twenty-eight years old in 1897, Boynton had been a soldier of fortune in South America for eight years and now, bearing the self-bestowed title of captain, lived in San Francisco. The usual plotlines followed: club members having a friendly argument, a boast made by Boynton, a wager proposed, his acceptance of the challenge of walking around the world within five years for $50,000 payable to the San Francisco charity of his choice. On August 11, Boynton set out on foot for New York. Like Jones, he started *au naturel* and without a cent. Also like Jones, he escaped nakedness by making a suit out of wrapping paper (quickly replaced, thanks to the largesse of a local clothier). Very much not like Jones, however, Boynton proposed to handle no money on the trek and to rely on the kindness of strangers to meet his needs. As he told a *Philadelphia Inquirer* reporter on February 11, 1898, he wanted to test whether "any man can go through the world without money and yet not be a hobo." That same month, he boarded an ocean liner (passage paid by a friend) for London, there to begin a freeloading tour of the British Isles.

Boynton's chutzpah didn't yield as good of results in Spain, with which the United States happened to be at war in 1898. When he finally reached the French border, he was so close to collapsing from starvation that he borrowed money to buy food. That, of course, ended the wager-walk, but no matter—he was eager to get on to another project: a scientific expedition to the North Pole via balloon.

For the June 15, 1898, issue of *Sketch* magazine, George Boynton modeled a paper suit like the one in which he began his long trek.

Returning to the United States in the spring of 1899, Boynton began a trek on June 26 from New York to San Francisco, hoping to find 5,000 "patriotic Americans" each willing to donate $10 to support his polar expedition. As usual, he would not seek or spend money for his expenses but also would not sleep in a bed or stay in hotels, except when in large cities. For sleep in cold or wet weather, he carried a "sleeping suit" of his own design. By October, he was in Colorado Springs, but an injury there to his knee ended his fundraising walk. Again, however, it didn't matter, because he had spotted a new field for exploitation: the mineral wealth of Colorado and Arizona. A succession of schemes followed in which investors lost money and one associate (but not Boynton) ended up in prison. Next came a failed scientific expedition to Brazil, truly valiant service in World War I, and a failed attempt to organize a scientific expedition to Central America (for this one, he became General Boynton).

The last two decades of Boynton's life are a mystery. Up to then, however, he had made his way charmingly by promoting dubious schemes and, as on his treks, tapping others for support. Many times he skipped out without paying money he owed, for which in one instance he went to prison for three months. Yet he clearly succeeded in being more than a hobo or a tramp; a better designation would be a con man.

Variations on a Theme

Following the lead of Paul Jones and George Melville Boynton, within the next fifteen years another dozen or so courageous souls attempted wager-walks that involved the wearing of temporary clothing made of paper. Both Jones and Boynton had fashioned their garments from wrapping paper, but thereafter others working this vein pinned together newspaper pages. (One used toothpicks to join pages taken from the *Police Gazette*.) However, a few trekkers began their journeys wearing the inexpensive paper clothes that could then be bought in some clothing stores. These suits looked presentable, but they didn't last long, and if rain came, disaster befell their occupants.

Hitting the trail in a paper suit attracted attention, but it was not necessarily a trek's only or most challenging feature. Consider, for instance, the odysseys of Frank Reilley and W. B. Jones, two of the last wager-walkers known to have worked the paper-suit angle.

Starting out as a Montana cowboy, Frank Reilley somehow ended up in 1908 at the age of twenty-eight involved in the following wager with the Meltentile Sporting Club of St. Louis. For a prize of $9,000 and a 10 percent cut of all bets, he would attempt to circle the globe within two and a half years traveling by foot, train, and ship. He would start out wearing a newspaper suit and possessing only one cent. He would not beg, borrow, steal, or ask for work, yet he would return with $500. The wager was clearly modeled on Paul Jones's except for one further feature: Reilley was required to get married while on the trip, but his bride must be the suitor and must ask him for his hand.

This adventure began on June 4, 1908, on the club's steps, where Reilley, wearing his newspaper suit, and a local tailor entered into an obviously prearranged deal: the tailor would provide Reilley with a high-quality cloth suit to replace his paper clothes on the condition that, at the end of the trek, he would return the cloth suit for the tailor's use in advertising. Reilley agreed, whereupon two blankets were held up behind which he changed clothes. He then tore his paper suit into small pieces and, buying a pencil with his one cent, autographed the fragments. From the sale of these souvenirs to the many people witnessing these antics, he cleared $92.50 for a good start to his trek.

Leaving on foot for San Francisco on June 6, 1908, Reilley kept moving

FRANK REILLEY.
Walking round the World without a penny
for wife and wager.

10,000 MILES ON FOOT WITHOUT A DOLLAR!
From Dallas, Texas, to Nome, Alaska
and return.
BUY A CARD -- GIVE WHAT YOU CAN
W. B. JONES

Likely the last trekkers to use the paper-suit gimmick, Frank Reilley
and W. B. Jones also made other big claims on their postcards.

west until he reached England in October of 1910. That didn't leave much time for getting to St. Louis by his deadline, and he still needed to garner $500. What sank the effort, however, was the marriage requirement. A newspaper reported that he had received "numerous proposals" along the way but had said yes to none.

W. B. Jones's challenge was to complete, within 400 walking days, a round trip between Dallas and Nome, Alaska, made mostly on foot but by ship between Seattle and Nome. The trek's prize was $10,000 posted by "four wealthy men in Texas and Oklahoma." The wager specified that Jones would start with a penny and in a paper suit, earn his own expenses as he traveled and not beg, and stay in the finest hotels available. Because he also had to reach each city broke, each time he left a city any unspent money was to be sent to an account whose balance would be doubled and paid to him at the end of the trek.

Wearing a crepe paper suit, Jones worked for a week in Dallas to earn money with which to buy a cloth suit. He left for Nome in late March of 1909, financing his trek by lecturing and singing in movie theaters and selling postcards on his way. In Bismarck, North Dakota, he sprained his ankle and was permitted to take the train from there to Sandpoint, Idaho, where, using crutches, he continued on foot to Seattle. Arriving there in November, he learned that navigation to Nome was closed for the winter. By unknown means he still got to Nome, where a bank teller gave him two collie dogs, Rover and Teddy.

By mid-January of 1910, Jones had reached Butte, Montana, on his return trek and was soon making good time on his way to Chicago and from there on to New Orleans. Not until early December was he back in Dallas, however—that is, about 200 days past the 400 days permitted for his trek. Although he had clearly lost the wager, accompanied by Rover and Teddy he proceeded to make thrilling presentations about their trek, illustrated by stereopticon views, in Texas movie houses.

Jones's story prompts some obvious questions that, regrettably, must remain unanswered. For instance, where did those stereopticon slides come from? Also, after making good time for so long, why did he fall so far off schedule in that last leg of his trek? And, most intriguing of all, why would anyone undertake a trip on foot that was scheduled to arrive almost to the Arctic Circle during the winter? At the very least, Jones rates high marks for audacity.

World's Champion Walker (Self-Proclaimed)

Although by the late 1880s pedestrianism had begun to decline as America's most popular professional sport, walking competitions claiming to offer big cash prizes and enlisting many competitors continued for several more decades. These events usually took place in large cities during the winter months. One of those contests was scheduled to begin in St. Louis shortly after New Year's Day in 1902. In anticipation of this six-day race, an article in the December 22, 1901, issue of the *St. Louis Republic* addressed a question that likely had not ever occurred to any of its readers, viz., how did professional pedestrians support themselves during the many off-season months?

The article's unidentified author found that "nearly all the important contestants have steady employment [in other fields] when not competing." The contenders in the forthcoming contest in St. Louis, for instance, included a real estate agent, a weaver, a stenographer, a carpenter, a blacksmith, and several athletic trainers, all of whom "adopt the sawdust patch in the winter merely because the sport is more profitable." Among the St. Louis registrants, however, the reporter found an exception: Harry J. West of Harrisburg, Pennsylvania, age twenty-seven and professionally known as Kid West, "confines himself entirely to this line of contests for a living, so far as is known."

Kid West was a top pedestrian competitor; in a six-day race held in Madison Square Garden in 1900, for instance, he completed over 500 miles and finished in third place. When he wasn't competing, he made long-distance treks, from which he presumably extracted additional income. His claimed long-distance completions included a trek around the world (28,000 miles, 29 months) and walks from Portland, Oregon, to New York (4,800 miles, 192 days), Quebec to Philadelphia (450 miles, 12 days), and Chicago to New York (908 miles, 27 days). This record, he claimed, established him as the champion long-distance walker of the world.

Regrettably, there is scant newspaper documentation or other evidence of the particulars or even the occurrences of West's claimed long-distance treks prior to a walk he made in 1900 from New York to San Francisco. According to West, that trek came about in the familiar manner: he and friends were discussing how long it would take a man

GOES ON A STROLL
TO SAN FRANCISCO

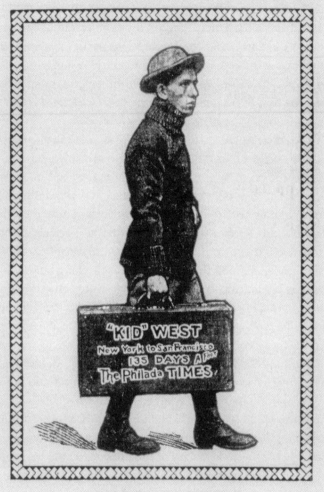

"KID" WEST ON HIS LONG TRAMP

Tramper West Starts on a Long Journey From
Camden to the Golden Gate.

Kid West's "stroll" got good coverage on August 2, 1900,
in the *Philadelphia Times*, a sponsor of his trek.

to walk from New York to San Francisco; West claimed he could do it in 135 days; one friend offered him a bet that he couldn't do it in that time; a $1,500 wager, plus posting of a purse of $500, soon followed. Once the trek was underway, however, the story began to change. His wager, West now claimed, was for $5,000 and made with Charles Morton, a friend in Kansas City. Then came yet another account that identified Morton and Kid Faro, a big-time gambler, as parties to a $5,000 wager (in one telling, $10,000), whose terms assured West of a liberal slice of the winnings if he completed the trek on time. One constant in these accounts was that $500 purse, which perhaps was the stake put up by another of the trek's sponsors, the *Police Gazette*.

West set out on August 1, 1900, from the *Police Gazette* offices on his long walk. Coverage of the trek by newspapers was ample but introduced further uncertainties. By one account, he was to spend no money and be totally "dependent on a generous public," and yet another account had him financing the trek by selling postcards. Then, the *Goodland (KS) Republic* on October 19 reported that he "was seen stealing a ride out of town on a freight train," but Reno's *Daily Nevada State Journal* on November 28 claimed that "a trotter travels along behind him and watches that he doesn't steal any forbidden rides." About one matter, however, newspapers concurred: the Kid was always decked out in golf knickers and a red sweater bearing the message "Kid West / New York to San Francisco / Police Gazette."

Upon reaching San Francisco on December 8, six and a half days ahead of his deadline, West made his usual claim to have set another record. For the next several years, he continued his pattern of following seasons of competitive walks with occasional long-distance treks. Although he acknowledged that his competitive record in 1902 was disappointing, he assured a reporter in February of 1903 that he would be a contender in an upcoming competition in Philadelphia. That was the last notice in the press, however, of Kid West, the self-proclaimed world's champion walker.

Monikers, Claims, and Titles

How and when Harry J. West happened to become Kid West is not known, but the fact that he adopted a sobriquet is not surprising. Many long-distance trekkers did so, another indication that their chosen field of endeavor smacked amply of show business. Some sported monikers having a western twang and coloration—examples are Dakota Bob, Montana Bob, Cherokee Buck, and Oklahoma Ed, all aspiring wager-walkers and low-tier showmen. Joining them on the road were other characters bearing such arresting names as Jack the Adventurer, Scotty the Newsboy, and Happy Jack or such self-bestowed titles as the Original Boy Tramp, the Cuban Wonder, and F. J. Cooper, the World's Wonder (inscribed on Cooper's back, this last message, according to one newspaper account, "attracts a good deal of attention on the streets," which was precisely the point).

Kid West's claim to be the world's champion long-distance walker was also a familiar boast made by wager-walkers. In the absence of official monitoring of competitions and recordkeeping, any claim could be asserted and then made "official" by constant repetition. Newspapers usually helped the trekkers' self-promotions by publishing their claims without bothering to check them out. The result was a proliferation of assertions of great achievement or unique standing—for instance, more than one trekker (some well past their eighteenth year) claimed to be the champion boy walker of the world, and at least one codger (eighty-one years old) put himself forward as the world's oldest trekker.

That long-distance wager-walking could get fully entangled with the glitzy realm of show-biz was well demonstrated by George H. Hayes, a thirty-year-old, 210-pound bodybuilder living in San Francisco. Hayes boxed, wrestled, and performed feats of strength in entertainment venues on the West Coast. He proclaimed himself to be not only the strongest man in the world but also the holder of world records in chest expansion (nine and three-fourths inches) and walking (seventy-five miles in fourteen hours, which, by his reckoning, topped Weston's best effort by three miles). On August 1, 1910, Hayes set out from San Francisco on a walk to New York, for which he claimed an unidentified sponsor would pay him $5,000 if he completed it within three years. That was a greater challenge than it might seem, because he was required, he said, to earn

Smiling Joe Callahan sold this postcard to finance his return trek to New York.

money in every town or city of at least 600 residents through which he trekked. How fortunate, then, that he could simply continue putting on shows that offered such claimed feats as breaking rocks with his hands, twisting horseshoes, and lifting a man by using only three fingers. For the trek, he also billed himself as Young Sandow, one of many tapping the luster of the world-famous strongman and showman Eugen Sandow. Upon reaching New York, Hayes planned to challenge Jack Johnson, the heavyweight boxing champ, to a match. He likely never got there, however; all evidence of Young Sandow ends with several articles appearing in Montana newspapers in December of that same year.

It would be hard to conjure up another long-distance trekker differing more starkly from Young Sandow than Joe Callahan, yet the latter was just as attentive to the need to fashion a unique walking persona. Although in his forties, Callahan presented himself as a New York City newsboy known as Smiling Joe. At five feet two and claiming to weigh only eighty-seven pounds, he plausibly purported to be the smallest long-distance pedestrian. Alleging to have walked over 35,000 miles in eleven years through Europe and South America, the frail-looking Callahan made the usual claim to be the world's champion walker. His most striking claim, however, was that he had learned to read and write on his walks!

On June 8, 1914, Smiling Joe began a trek from New York to San Francisco on a $6,000 wager allegedly made by his father, a big shot in Tammany Hall, with a former New York City sheriff. Upon arrival in San Francisco on December 22, he announced that the walk was only half done, and on April 22, 1915, he began a return trek to New York. To cover expenses, he lectured and did wrestling matches in theaters with his dog, Doc Snookums. Later, Doc was replaced by Trix, who was touted as the only dog ever to carry Old Glory in his jaws on a cross-country trek. Because Smiling Joe and Trix are known to have reached Tyrone, Pennsylvania, on March 1, 1916, it's likely they got to New York by their June 1 deadline.

Early Teams of Two

In the nineteenth century, cross-country wager-walkers were almost exclusively males; among the rare exceptions were Zoe Gayton and the mother-and-daughter team of Helga and Clara Estby. Wager-walking was then also mainly a solitary activity—most trekkers walked alone. The handful of exceptions included, once again, the Estbys; a married couple named John and Lulu Howard; and three duos of male trekkers, only one of which—Morris Cohen and Frank Polk—got very far.

John and Lulu Howard were variety-show actors in Seattle who, in 1892, set out to walk from that city to Chicago. John was forty-seven and Lulu forty. They had been approached about making this trek by Perry Burns, who owned the theater in which they performed and was also, according to a Seattle newspaper article, a "millionaire liquor dealer." After making a large bet on the trek with a sporting man in San Francisco, Burns secured the Howards' participation by offering to pay them $5,000 upon the trek's completion. It was too good an offer to turn down.

The Howards took off on March 10, following railroad lines most of the way and needing to reach Chicago no later than September 15 to collect their prize. Their agreement with Burns required that they camp out and never stay in a hotel or other building; walk all the way, never traveling by other means; register with railroad stationmasters at all cities and towns on their route; and cover their expenses by earning money as they traveled. (They met this last requirement by performing their song-and-dance routines in local theaters—one more instance of the easy merger of trekking with show business.) To ensure compliance with these requirements, the parties to the wager hired a Mr. J. B. Morrison to follow the Howards by train and occasionally descend upon them unannounced.

To carry their tent, clothes, and supplies—about a hundred pounds in all—John had built a wheelbarrow that Lulu pulled while he pushed when they encountered rough roads. What really got the attention of newspapers, however, was the fact that Lulu wore men's clothes. That made good sense, but it was shocking and unprecedented. Zoe Gayton had even forgone wearing bloomers in favor of donning full-length woolen dresses, and four years after the Howards' trek, the new-model garments that the Estbys wore were still ample dresses. As many news-

Peddling copies of this photo, Morris Cohen and Frank Polk
trekked west until kayoed by an early blizzard in Nebraska.

papers noted, Lulu's clothing and diminutive size made her look like a boy. Around the start of the trek, on April 2, 1892, the *Dalles (OR) Times-Mountaineer* speculated that when Lulu "appears in Eastern cities, in her male attire, there may be trouble, and she may be forced, for the sake of propriety, to don her skirts and dress." No trouble or scandal is known to have happened, however, and the Howards arrived in Chicago on August 31, fifteen days before their deadline. Mr. Morrison, their tracker, was there to greet them and to hand them a check for $5,000.

Less successful were Morris Cohen and Frank Polk, who on June 9, 1897, left Jersey City on foot for San Francisco; if they got there by January 7, they would share a $5,000 bet, and they would get another $2,500 if they arrived by Christmas Day. Accompanied by two large dogs— Denver and Frisco—the men pushed wheelbarrows bearing American flags and carrying camping gear and supplies.

To finance the trek, they planned to sell their photographs and exhibit themselves in rented halls as they traveled. That latter option was not as absurd or unpromising as it sounds. As documented by numerous newspaper clippings, these men made a huge splash, everywhere being "accorded great receptions" and "treated as heroes," according to the *Jersey City News* on August 7, 1897. Both were about thirty years old, army veterans, handsome, and "fine specimens of physical perfection," in the judgment of the June 15, 1897, *Newark Daily Advocate*, which added that they were also intelligent and good talkers. They professed to be taking notes to use later in writing a book about their trek.

By early September, they were at Burlington, Iowa, still claiming to be having a great time. The *Burlington Evening Gazette* on September 7, 1897, judged otherwise, however: "The men are considerably weather-beaten and seemed to be having a rather rough road to travel." Pressing on, they reached western Nebraska by late October, where, near Ogallala, they ran into a freakish early snowstorm of great severity. "Since then life hasn't been worth living" for them, reported Nebraska's *Lincoln State Journal* on October 28. That was their last newspaper notice, and likely it also marked the end of their trek.

The Khaki Kids

Teams of two trekkers became commonplace, perhaps even the norm, during the years of trekking's greatest vogue in the early twentieth century. Some of those pairings were brothers or, following the lead of John and Lulu Howard, married couples, who in a few instances brought along young children. Most of the trekking duos, however, were friends of the same gender—sometimes female pairs, but much more often teams of two young men. A colorful example was Charles Hahn and Walter Chaffee, who billed themselves as the Khaki Kids in recognition of their trekking attire.

Hahn hailed from Richmond, Virginia, and Chaffee from Buffalo, New York. A newspaper reported that both were students at the University of Pennsylvania and twenty-one years old in 1909. That happened also to be the year in which Edward Payson Weston attempted to walk from New York to San Francisco in a hundred days. After listening to friends discuss admiringly Weston's well-publicized effort, Hahn and Chaffee were not impressed. Making no allowances for the fact that Weston was then seventy years old, they boasted, as one newspaper account put it, that they or "almost any well-preserved man" could do what Weston was attempting. That led, of course, to a challenge, and soon the young men were committed to making a timed walk across the United States for a $1,000 prize.

Their trek would reach from Philadelphia to Seattle, which in 1909 was the host city of a world's fair, the Alaska-Yukon-Pacific Exposition. As laid out by the sports editor of the *Philadelphia Inquirer*, the trek's route came to nearly 4,000 miles. Hahn and Chaffee would have 137 days to cover this distance, which meant that they would need to average twenty-nine miles a day. To assure that they followed the specified route, the trekkers were required to secure a signed affidavit from the mayor or other official of every city of 10,000 or more residents on the route. Other requirements included that they each carry eighteen to twenty pounds of personal luggage in a knapsack; start without a cent; neither beg, borrow, steal, nor work for money; stay every night in the best available hotel; and obtain money to cover expenses solely from the sale of postcards.

Starting from Philadelphia on May 18, 1909, the Khaki Kids faced a

SOUVENIR OF THE TWO WALKERS ON A $1,000 WAGER
FROM PHILADELPHIA TO SEATTLE IN 137 DAYS

As recorded on their postcard, pith helmets top off the trekking duds worn
by Charles Hahn and Walter Chaffee, the self-designated Khaki Kids.

deadline of October 1 for arrival in Seattle. To add a touch of excitement to their drab khaki uniforms, they donned tall white pith helmets of the kind used by the British army. The trekkers stayed on roads until reaching Aberdeen, South Dakota, in late July, but then they followed railroad tracks. As required by their contract, they always stayed in first-class hotels, except for thirteen occasions when they were accommodated in ranch houses. Their travel expenses averaged $4 per day, which amount they had no difficulty raising by the sale of postcards. (They sometimes also performed a vaudeville comic act in theaters along the way, skirting the ban on working for money by tying performances in some way to the sale of postcards.)

As Hahn and Chaffee moved west, favorable newspaper accounts of them and their expedition piled up. Articles often noted that they appeared to be in top physical condition; an account published in the *Anaconda (MT) Standard* on August 30, 1909, for instance, described them as "hearty as a pair of bucks." Confirming the newspapers' attribution of their great athletic prowess, the trekkers reached Seattle on September 26, five days ahead of their deadline. In fact, their achievement was even more impressive than that. Of their trek's 131 lapsed days, rain had made it impossible to walk on 39 of them. That left only ninety-two days for walking, yielding an average of forty-three miles per walking day—an exceptionally good rate to maintain over the trek's long distance.

Hahn and Chaffee reported that the roads they used were generally in good condition. It takes no luster from their achievement to note that other trekkers often found that not to be so; Cohen and Polk, for instance, encountered roads impaired by flooding in Illinois and closed by a blizzard in Nebraska. Evidence that the Khaki Kids' trek was charmed was the astonishing statement they made to a reporter for Montana's *Daily Missoulian* on September 29, 1909, that "the finest roads we found were in Iowa. The roads in that state were excellent." No one had ever said that before! Indeed, in the judgment of most motorists, Iowa's roads, sitting atop a rich gumbo soil, were the worst in the nation. The Khaki Kids, however, did their best walking in Iowa, claiming even eighty miles on one day.

A Family Project

During cross-country trekking's golden years, from the opening of the twentieth century to America's entry into World War I, trekkers often moved in groups larger than two. Three-person expeditions and even teams of four trekkers were sometimes afoot—Boy Scouts taking a long hike to earn merit badges, for instance, or fraternal lodge brothers hoofing their way to a national conclave. Likely unique, however, was a cross-country effort attempted in 1908 by five male trekkers, all of whom also had a close family connection.

The five participants in this unusual family project were three brothers, Louis, Peter, and John Marsouin, twenty-one, eighteen, and sixteen years old, respectively; their cousin, whose name happened to be Louis Cousin, circa twenty-two; and their uncle, Victor Allo, about thirty. French Canadians in origin, all were then residents of Cranford, New Jersey, where all were employed as landscapers or gardeners.

How so many members of this family were inclined to take a cross-country jaunt is not known, but the trek's origin involved the familiar features of an argument among friends about a trek, boasts by some, a challenge laid down by others, and the passing of the hat to raise money for a wager. In this instance, the amount was $1,000 to be shared equally by anyone completing the trek from Cranford to San Francisco. (However, later newspaper accounts put it at $500 per participant.) The trekkers were required to start with no funds and to cover their expenses by earning money or receiving freely offered food and lodging (no begging permitted) as they traveled. Each carried a knapsack holding his clothing and cooking and eating utensils. No deadline was specified.

On April 14, 1908, well-wishers in Cranford gave the trekkers a rousing send-off, which was followed later that day by a hearty reception and lunch in Plainfield. The next day, in New Brunswick, Louis and John lamented that they had become separated from the others, but by April 17 all five were together again as they reached Trenton. Sometime after entering Pennsylvania, however, the team of five underwent a longer-lasting disaggregation into three parts—a solo Victor Allo, a duo comprised of cousins Peter Marsouin and Louis Cousin, and the remaining two trekkers, the brothers Louis and John Marsouin. Both Allo and the team of two cousins soon began selling postcards to finance

VICTOR ALLO
WALKING FROM NEW JERSEY TO SAN FRANCISCO
WITHOUT A CENT

PETER MARSOUIN and LOUIS COUSIN
Walking from Cranford, N. J. to San Francisco

Victor Allo and his nephews (two shown here) left New Jersey
for San Francisco, but likely they didn't get past Kansas.

their separate treks. That those postcards were so readily available for this purpose suggests that their sellers' original commitment to stick with the group may not have been a wholehearted one. By late May, however, the two cousins had reconnected with the two brothers in Indiana, and thereafter the four trekkers stayed together for the rest of the journey. Victor Allo continued to move west alone.

How did they fare? On October 22, 1908, the *Lawrence (KS) Daily World* published this account of their treks: "April 14th they left . . . on their long tramp, keeping together until they reached Pittsburg, Pa. Here the uncle, Victor Allo, left them and went on ahead, making twice as fast a pace as they, and reached San Francisco this summer. He won his $500, which was promptly paid and he returned and joined the other three [*sic*] who were slowly working their way westward, near Lawrence, about the middle of the summer. The parties [in New Jersey], with whom they had made the wager, were now convinced that the boys would make good and agreed to compromise on $250 and let the boys stop their walk in Kansas. This the boys agreed to and the long walk ended near Williamstown."

The *Daily World*'s claims that Allo reached San Francisco during the summer and received $500 were almost certainly false; earlier articles in other newspapers had him still in Iowa in late June. That those placing the wager concluded that they would lose and so proposed to settle for a lesser amount also sounds dubious. Indeed, the only solid fact here may be that the participants' treks had come to an end in eastern Kansas in mid- to late summer. Very likely, too, they were glad to be done with the project; according to the *Daily World* article, Allo and two of the boys "at once took a Pullman" back to New Jersey. However, two of the Marsouin brothers—Peter and Louis—were fetched by the bucolic charms of Kansas and found farmwork there. Unfortunately, staying in Kansas proved to be a fateful decision for Peter: exiting a barn on a farm near Lawrence in October, he was struck by lightning and instantly killed.

Some Boys from Pittsburgh

Although money was the usual object of the wager-walkers, in a few instances other items of value were the incentive and the goal. That was so for the walk attempted by two brothers from Pittsburgh—James Walter Dyer, twenty-four, and Elmer Ellsworth Dyer, twenty-two—who on June 15, 1915, set out from that city to walk to San Francisco on the understanding that they would take no money and meet all their expenses by selling postcards of themselves and doing odd jobs; if they got to San Francisco by September 15, each would receive a four-year scholarship to any of the state universities of Pennsylvania. Posting this offer was Charles Strather of Wilkinsburg, Pennsylvania, identified in newspapers as a wealthy coal mine owner for whom both Dyer brothers had once worked. According to the *Eau Claire (WI) Leader* on August 8, 1915, "Mr. Strather's hobby is endurance feats of all kinds and he is paying many a boy's way through college for fulfilling the requirements of his tests." The Dyer brothers probably never made it onto that list of beneficiaries, however; all newspaper evidence of their westward progress ends with this article.

Seven years earlier, two other young men—E. F. "Feathers" Gage, twenty-five years old, and H. F. "Dusty" Flynn, twenty-four years old—also departed from Pittsburgh on a wager-walk in pursuit of another out-of-the-ordinary prize. To the *Abilene (KS) Daily Reporter* of December 22, 1908, they gave these details. Unable to find work, they resolved to go to South Dakota to stake a claim but, lacking money for railroad fares, decided to proceed on foot, working their way there. Flynn's uncle, John F. Coyle, a real estate mogul in Pittsburgh and Chicago, tried to dissuade them by offering to pay their tuition for four years if they enrolled in college. That effort failing, Coyle, allegedly in jest, proposed that they make their jaunt a round-the-world trek for a big prize. Surprised that they showed strong interest, he was soon discussing the features of such a trip with them. From these talks came his agreement to provide each, upon successful completion of the trek, with a 500-acre farm (plus money to stock it) located anywhere in the United States.

To claim these munificent prizes, Feathers and Dusty would have five years to complete a tour around the world following an itinerary drawn up by Coyle in which they would visit "every Nation That Floats a Navy."

E. R. ("FEATHERS") GAGE   H. F. ("DUSTY") FLYNN
OF BINGHAMPTON, N.Y.   OF PITTSBURG, PA.
LEFT PITTSBURG EXPOSITION, 9:00 P. M., SEPT. 7, 1906 TO TOUR
THE WORLD ON FOOT IN FIVE YEARS, VISITING EVERY
NATION THAT FLOATS A NAVY.

The Dyer brothers and Feathers and Dusty, like many
other trekkers, favored military-style khaki clothing.

The tour would total 50,000 miles, of which 27,000 would be covered on foot and the remainder done by boat or ship. They would leave without money and would meet all expenses on the journey, including ocean passage, by working and selling postcards of themselves. Each day when on land they would send a postcard to Chicago, and once every week they would mail a fuller account of their experiences and condition to Pittsburgh. Never explained was a final requirement that they not cut their hair during the five years they were on this trip (although they were permitted to shave).

Accepting these terms, the young pedestrians left on September 7, 1908, from the grounds of the then happening Pittsburgh Exposition amid the cheers of 12,000 fairgoers. Within two months, they were in western Nebraska, where they swerved in a southwest direction to go through Kansas, New Mexico, and Arizona. By early February, they were in Los Angeles and soon reached San Francisco. They had averaged thirty-two miles per day of walking in this first phase of their trek; now came the next phase, travel by ship to the Philippines and then on to Japan.

Except that didn't happen. Instead, the boys were soon walking back in the direction from which they had just come. As they explained to a reporter in Cheyenne, after securing jobs on a ship, they learned that they needed to join a union to hold those jobs, but paying union dues would violate the restriction they were under not to pay for passage across the ocean. After spending several fruitless days looking for work with other shipping companies, they concluded that they might have better luck with companies crossing the Atlantic Ocean, so they set out for New York City on foot.

Clearly, much was flimsy in their reasoning, but perhaps they were having second thoughts about being gone from the United States for the next four and a half years. Indeed, they may soon have soured on the whole project, because no evidence can be found that the trek lasted beyond their arrival in Indiana in late June of 1909. By then, too, they had already gone nine months without haircuts.

For Love and Money

On October 25, 1912, two longtime close friends—Walter Standow, age twenty-five, and Henry Danes, age twenty-seven—set out from New York on a wager-walk to San Francisco. Bound by the familiar provisions that they start without a cent and not beg, borrow, steal, or work for money, they also planned to follow the common practice of meeting their expenses by selling postcards. If they completed their trek within eight months, they claimed, they would collect a $2,000 prize posted by Standow's uncle, who had also made a $10,000 bet on the trek. Soon newspaper accounts had that cash prize ranging as high as $8,000, and the rich uncle's largesse had somehow also expanded to include three years of tuition for the lads at New York's Columbia Journalism School (then called the Pulitzer School). Whatever the true facts were, however, likely no feature of their trek was unprecedented—that is, until they reached Johnstown, Pennsylvania.

In Johnstown, the trekkers chanced to meet a Miss Sylvia Thorpe, and they were so smitten by her charms that each extended a marriage proposal to her. For her part, she was attracted to both men and couldn't decide which offer to accept. At that point, Miss Thorpe's father had a great idea: why not let his daughter's hand in marriage be a prize awarded to the winner of a walking contest from Johnstown to St. Louis? All parties agreeing to this novel proposal, the two trekkers took off for Missouri, no longer partners but now competitors. The winner was Henry Danes, and on December 30 three St. Louis newspapers reported that his marriage to Miss Thorpe would take place in that city within several days.

That didn't happen. Claiming to learn that his walking contract had somehow been breached, Danes now said that he had to put the wedding on hold and walk back to New York. If he arrived there by May 1, having also completed 4,500 trekking miles, he would collect a $6,000 prize, plus that three-year scholarship (which he now alleged was offered by his future father-in-law). Once back in New York, he would also proceed to marry Miss Thorpe. What must she have thought, then, when Danes next announced that the wedding would have to wait until he completed his three-year college program?

Meanwhile, the heartsick Walter Standow assumed that he and Danes would continue to trek together to California. Any possibility of that

WALTER STANDOW
OF EAU CLAIRE, WIS.
WALKING FROM
NEW YORK TO 'FRISCO
FOR A COLLEGE EDUCATION, AS A REWARD.

"FRISCO SPOT" THE GREATEST LITTLE "DOG GLOBE TROTTER" IN THE WORLD FAITHFULLY ACCOMPANIES HIM ON HIS TRIP.

STARTED—HERALD SQUARE, NEW YORK CITY   DUE—SAN FRANCISCO, CAL.
OCTOBER 25, 1912.   JUNE 25, 1913.

Although Walter Standow did get from New York to San Francisco on foot, his trek included some highly novel features not indicated on his postcard.

happening ended, however, after Danes mockingly confirmed Standow's suspicion that Danes had cheated. According to Standow, a fistfight ensued, after which both combatants ended up in the St. Louis jail. Upon his release, Danes did head back to New York and a sad Standow continued walking to San Francisco, now accompanied by Frisco Spot, a fox terrier.

When he reached Jefferson City, Missouri, Standow's spirits lifted. Awaiting him there was a letter bringing joyous news. As it happened, word of Danes's cheating had gotten out, and when his bride-to-be learned of it, she was done with Danes, and in her letter she conveyed her promise to marry Standow. Thereafter, in statements to the press, Standow affirmed that upon completion of his trek he would marry the lady whose hand he had won in a footrace—Eva Hallam, an employee of a photo studio in Pittsburgh. But hold on: wasn't that young lady Sylvia Thorpe of Johnstown? Then in May came yet more confusion: as reported in several newspapers, the future bride was now Mabel Wilton of Johnstown! By the time Standow's trek was over, Eva had recovered her standing over Mabel in his statements to the press, but poor Sylvia never once got a mention.

As Standow moved west, other claimed features of his trek also evolved. In the story's original telling, for instance, upon the trek's completion a rich uncle would bestow $2,000 upon Standow and pay his tuition for three years at the Pulitzer School. In later accounts, however, $3,000 was the amount he would be paid at the trek's conclusion for weekly accounts sent to a publisher in Germany. The uncle was still on for paying for the scholarship, but now, to receive it, Standow had to complete the trek by a certain (unspecified) date.

Standow reached San Francisco on July 16, 1913. After having trekked for nine months, he reported being three weeks too late to get that scholarship. Also, the $3,000 vanished with the German publisher's purported bankruptcy. But did he get the maiden? If so, let's hope that she was the right one.

"Women Westons Walk"

In July of 1910, many American newspapers carried a syndicated article touting seven "Women Now in the News." Praised for their bold ventures or achievements were three pioneer aviators (this was 1910!), a circus clown, a champion butter maker, and two women then engaged in walking from their hometown of Muskogee, Oklahoma, to San Francisco. The walkers were characterized as "emulating Weston," who was then on his walk from Los Angeles to New York and was much in the news. Several other newspapers also linked the two women to the famous pedestrian; the *San Antonio Light and Gazette*, for instance, on May 26, 1910, headlined its coverage succinctly as "Women Westons Walk."

The "Women Westons" were Bessie S. Jenkins and Carrie T. Seery, but only a few newspapers, all in the Far West, identified them by those names. In all other newspapers, in line with the standard journalistic practice of that day, they were Mrs. Charles Smith Jenkins and Mrs. Frank J. Seery. Although no articles revealed their ages, most described them as young, and all reported that both were college graduates making the trek for their own edification and enjoyment. Jenkins was identified as a sketch artist and Seery as a former newspaper writer. To finance their trek, they claimed to have contracted with the *St. Louis Post-Dispatch* and the *Chicago Examiner* to send in sketches and articles as they traveled. They also planned to write a book about their trek based on these sketches and articles. They had no schedule or deadline but expected the trek would take at least three months.

These were the trek's features as announced on March 10, but by month's end most had been shoved aside by a radically different plan: the women would walk for big money—to be precise, $25,000. How this dramatic change came about is not known, but Seery's sister appears to have put up most of the money backing the trekkers, while the other side of the wager was taken by a "traveling man" and others who declined to be identified. Although no deadline was specified, the trekkers were required to make a "continuous" journey having "no unnecessary delays," to send weekly dispatches to the *Muskogee Times-Democrat*, and to meet their expenses solely by selling postcards.

In early April, Jenkins and Seery began training by walking six miles a day; by the end of the month, they had gotten their daily quota up to

The postcards prepared by Bessie Jenkins and Carrie Seery let all viewers know that they trekked well armed.

eighteen miles. They also commissioned a tailor to create durable and comfortable trekking clothes that would meet the standards of the day for decorum and femininity. What resulted were tan-colored costumes clearly following in fashion the practical "new style garment" pioneered by Helga and Clara Estby in 1896—boots, leggings, full sleeves, but slightly shorter and less billowy skirts. Eschewing the small caps worn by the Estbys, the Muskogee women settled upon larger, sombrero-like hats. In another stylistic departure, they would each wear a loose-fitting gun belt from which a holstered .45 caliber revolver prominently dangled. They then hired a local photography studio to prepare 5,000 postcards depicting them in their trekking garb. (Seery's name is misspelled on those postcards, however.)

In the early morning of May 4, 1910, a large crowd gathered in front of the offices of the *Muskogee Times-Democrat* to bid farewell to the "Women Westons." The trekkers departed at 8:30 a.m. but not before selling enough postcards, at two for twenty-five cents, to bring in $5. By day's end, they had garnered another $5 from postcard sales and figured their total expenses for the day at only $1.30. Clearly, they would have no difficulty financing their trek. By having more postcards shipped as needed to rail stations along their route, they could count on always having an ample supply to fill the deep pockets of their skirts. Because they followed railroad tracks and shipped their suitcases each day to the place where they planned to spend the night, they could travel lightly, each carrying only a blanket in addition to her six-shooter and day's supply of postcards.

On October 1, almost five months after their departure, the trekkers reached San Francisco. They had covered 2,385 miles in seventy-nine walking days for an average of 31 miles per day. Although no newspaper recorded the fact, presumably the trekkers collected the $25,000, which had been on deposit and guaranteed. Getting that money seems, too, to have been a matter of special importance to their husbands; as one of them told the *Checotah (OK) Times* of April 29, 1910, "If the girls can pull down $25,000 . . . they will have enough to buy them automobiles and bungalows."

Trekking While Black

The August 23, 1904, issue of the *Wisconsin State Journal* carried an intriguing account of one J. Mott, a Black man from Australia, age forty-two, who claimed to be passing through Madison on a 4,976-mile walk that had been laid out by a sports club in San Francisco. The walk began in that latter city on March 1 and would end by December 1 in New York. Competing against Mott was a Swede, Isaac Toetiol, who was sponsored by a different San Francisco club; his route to New York was of identical length to Mott's but followed a more southerly path. The sponsoring clubs had posted prize money totaling $12,000, of which 80 percent would go to the winner and the remainder to the loser. Each contender would get $21 per week for expenses. Mott would also receive a share of $42,000 allegedly won by some sporting men in a side bet made on a segment of his trek. Mott's wife and child, whom he had not seen for a year and a half, would meet him on his stop in Detroit and join him again in New York, after which the family would return to Australia, far richer than when they had come to America.

A charming story, but it doesn't ring true. Among its earmarks of a bogus trekking account are its implausible big-money claims and its premise that two sports clubs would bring two foreign nationals to the United States to engage in an expensive competition that ran for nine months far beyond the clubs' direct oversight and control. Such a contest would also have drawn the attention of the press, yet no newspaper articles about it seem to have been published other than the one aforementioned article. Too, that lone article described Mott's trek as proceeding swimmingly, providing no hint of any of the risks that a Black man walking alone across America would have faced at that time. In sum, without more details and documentation, Mott's story seems too wobbly to accept.

Would any Black man or woman in the early twentieth century have even attempted a cross-country walk or kept at it for very long after starting out? The odds surely weighed against either event, yet newspaper archives yield evidence of a handful of long-distance walks by Black trekkers, usually in pursuit of alleged cash prizes. Two of those trekkers were James A. Waters and Nebrasker Williams.

James Waters arrived in Dubuque, Iowa, in late June of 1915, claiming

World's Champion Walkers and Explorers

MR. and MRS. NEBRASKER WILLIAMS and "BIG BOY"

Now walking around the world. We two have the history of our lives from 5 years old. We are going to publish a book at the end of our journey. We also will receive $25,000 and a scholarship. Up to date we have walked 18,000 miles, starting on June 4, 1926, at Shreveport, La. If you have anything to give, give it to us. We are trying to make a record.

AROUND THE GLOBE IN 5 YEARS
PRICE 15 CENTS

A blotter sold by Nebrasker Williams and his wife presents some dubious claims about their treks. Photo courtesy of Kenneth Wilson.

to have covered 2,260 miles on foot since setting out from Philadelphia on April 10. According to the *Dubuque Telegraph Herald* of June 23, 1915, Waters was walking on a wager of $400 and needed to reach Denver within 160 days of his departure. He was identified as an "artist" who "does some of his work to pay his expenses." Waters must not have encountered any out-of-the-ordinary impediments to his trek, because the *Morgan County Republican* of Brush, Colorado, reported his arrival there on August 6, only seventy miles short of his Denver destination and more than a month ahead of his deadline. Very likely, he would go on to complete the trek and win the wager.

Then there was Nebrasker Williams. In 1927, this twenty-two-year-old resident of Shreveport, Louisiana, walked from there to Boston, allegedly in pursuit of a $1,000 prize. Soon after starting, as reported by the *Richmond (VA) Planet* on December 17, 1927, he was "stopped by a mob, shot in the leg, and put to work on the levee"; escaping after three days, he went on to win the prize and trek back to Shreveport early in 1928. He would use his prize, he announced, to finance the study of law at the University of Michigan. By that fall, however, he was off on another trek, this one, by his claim, worldwide in scope for a $50,000 prize; he was accompanied by his sister and a newly acquired wife. Drawing much hostile attention in Louisiana, they were arrested and sent to a prison farm, but after a month there, again by Williams's account, they escaped using a cell key that Mrs. Williams had fashioned out of a spoon. Between October of 1928 and March of 1930, newspaper accounts place the trio in Indianapolis, Los Angeles, and Baltimore, but their newspaper coverage ceased for the entire decade of the 1930s.

From 1931 to 1937, Williams later claimed to have trekked through fifty-one countries. No longer married to his first wife, it appears, in 1936 he wed Sheena, billed as a "Zulu princess." With her, he came back to the United States in 1937 and continued walking through 1942. In 1948, he resumed walking in quest of donations with which to buy salt and soap for a mission he had started in the Belgian Congo. When last heard from in 1951, he was the Reverend Nebrasker Williams and still walking for African causes.

The Student Pedestrian

In a category all by himself was another Black long-distance trekker, one Charles Henry Foster. Other trekkers walked in quest of mere cash prizes, but Foster aimed at something loftier and potentially more valuable—namely, an education at Harvard University. At least, that's what he steadily asserted, though how trekking would lead to the realization of that objective was not at all evident, and no reporter ever bothered to ask him for clarification. Nonetheless, his claim to be the student pedestrian headed for Harvard seemed to be generally accepted and to serve his trekking well.

Accounts of Foster's background are meager. In 1910, he told a reporter that he grew up in Texas as one of twelve siblings, moved with two brothers to Chicago, and was somewhere "between 22 and 25 years old." Reporters failed to disclose what his work was in Chicago, but one did identify him as a student there, and several noted that he was an "amateur marathon runner." Foster expanded his involvement in long-distance athletic activities on July 27, 1910, when he took off on a round-trip walk between Chicago and Portland, Maine. He carried with him a letter of greeting and introduction from Chicago's mayor to the mayor of Portland, but why that city was his destination is not known. Although he expected to complete his round trip in forty-five days, he encountered so much heavy rain that he had only reached Portland in that stretch of time, and the return trek took even longer.

Despite the many rain delays, the trek went well for Foster, whose likable features and easygoing manner usually assured him a good reception. One reporter noted that Foster "wears a golden smile," and another observed in the *Goshen (IN) Democrat* on November 1, 1910, that "Foster is a bright, cheery fellow and makes friends everywhere he goes." That reporter also noted that Foster "does not ask for money or help nor does he lodge at the finest hotel, but just takes things as they come and eats whatever he can find on the road and sleeps when he gets tired." Of course, had Foster tried to register at "the finest hotel" (or almost any other) on the way, he likely would have been refused. As reported by the *Syracuse Post-Standard* on October 24, 1910, he slept in "haystacks and barns" and carried with him "an alarm clock to awaken him in the morning before farmers are likely to get up and find him."

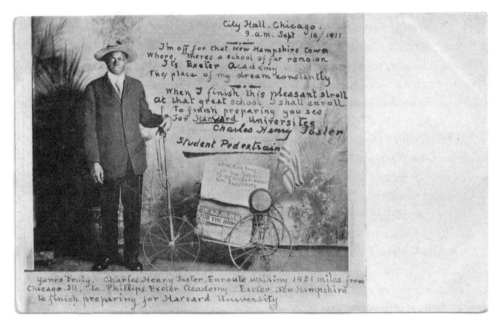

Charles Henry Foster's postcard lays out his plan for trekking to high educational attainment.

Always stressing that he was not walking to win a wager, collect a cash prize, set a record, or win fame, Foster instead purported to be trekking for experience, improved athletic ability, or sheer pleasure. Always, too, he let it be known that in the coming year, 1911, he would enroll at Harvard University. As he neared Chicago on his return trip, Foster informed reporters for several newspapers that he believed he might even receive a scholarship to Harvard in recognition of the athletic prowess demonstrated by his successful trek. In any case, as he told the reporter for the *Syracuse Post-Standard*, "I haven't a cent, but I am as confident of graduating from Harvard as though I was Rockefeller's son."

When the fall of 1911 arrived, Foster was headed east again on a walking expedition—not to Cambridge, Massachusetts, and Harvard University, however, but to Exeter, New Hampshire, where, he announced, he would enroll in Phillips Exeter Academy to prepare for admission to Harvard. He pulled a three-wheeled vehicle that carried his clothing, personal supplies, and a large batch of postcards that featured his picture, a poem of his own composition, and his self-identification as the "student pedestrain." By November 8, he had reached Boston and was soon in Exeter. At least two newspaper articles, one with an Exeter dateline, recorded that he was, in fact, admitted to the academy. Then, according to several newspaper accounts, to get money to continue his studies, in the summer of 1912 Foster set out on foot for Montreal to work temporarily in the dining cars of the Canadian Pacific Railway. But that, alas, ends the newspaper trail of Charles Henry Foster, the student pedestrian.

Did Foster ever get to Harvard? Weighing against that outcome was an announcement in a Boston newspaper in 1917 indicating that Charles Henry Foster, "the colored heavyweight of Chicago, wants to get some bouts here" and "show the fans what he can do." Then, a syndicated story appearing in 1921 reported that Foster, "the student globe trotter who has walked almost all over the world," was struck by a car as he took off from New York to San Francisco, aiming at a record time of sixty days.

Skating to Frisco

On May 9, 1910, Abe Levine took off from New York's City Hall on his roller skates and headed up Broadway, hoping to reach Yonkers by nightfall as the first stop on a trip to San Francisco. His friend Max Brody accompanied him on a bicycle, hauling their luggage and supplies. Cross-country treks by bicycle had been done before, but very likely Levine's was the original attempt to roller-skate across the country (more attempts would come in the next dozen years; see chapter 5 for some examples). Both trekkers were dressed nattily in red sweaters, red skating caps, and gray trousers.

Levine and Brody, sixteen-year-old high school students living in Paterson, New Jersey, were enthusiastic, expert bicyclists and roller skaters. Their decision to make a cross-country jaunt seems to have been born solely of youthful exuberance, thirst for adventure, and the desire to demonstrate their athletic prowess. They were not responding to the challenge of a wager or the promise of a prize, nor was any adult sponsorship, guidance, or supervision involved (although they did carry a letter of introduction from the Paterson YMCA, which they used to solicit support from local YMCAs).

Aiming to reach San Francisco in one hundred days (not counting Sundays, holidays, and rainy days), the boys expected to cover their costs by giving exhibitions of fancy skating and trick bicycle riding. That they started out with only thirty-five cents between them showed their supreme self-confidence—or, perhaps more accurately stated, revealed an astonishing naivete about what likely lay ahead. Although Levine used skates specially prepared for travel on rough roads, a *New York Tribune* reporter present at their departure observed on May 10 that the young men "seemed to have no idea of the bad roads which have been encountered by others in a coast-to-coast journey. They had absolute confidence in the skates and the bicycle, which was weighted down to the limit with an emergency outfit." Edward Payson Weston, just one week finished with his seventy-five-day trek from Los Angeles to New York, happened to be at City Hall at the time of their departure. Although he saw the boys off, the reporter noted, he "did not offer them any advice." Perhaps Weston also took a dim view of their prospects.

Hard-pressed financially from the start and broke by the time they

New York to San Francisco on Rollers

YOUNG'S SKATES NEW YORK

ABE LEVINE AND MAX BRODY, NEW YORK

Abe Levine and Max Brody made the first attempt to roller-skate across the country.

reached Albany, Levine and Brody quit trekking there for three days to replenish their finances by doing farmwork. In Buffalo, they gave a skating exhibition and used their earnings to procure a supply of postcards to sell as they continued west. Their depictions on the postcards revealed that two big changes to their trek had already occurred: first, Brody no longer rode a bicycle but instead joined Levine in making the trip on roller skates (how they transported luggage and supplies thereafter is not known) and, second, their trip now had a sponsor, the Young Roller Skate Manufacturing Company, indicated by the words "Young's / Skates / New York" emblazoning their sweaters.

How Young company officials learned of the boys' trek is not known, but why they would take an interest in it is clear. The company maintained a Young Skaters Club for youthful users of its skates. The company's obvious promotional course of action was to put Levine and Brody on Young skates and announce that the boys, now members of the club, were contending for a big prize—in this instance, $2,000—to be awarded by the club if they got to San Francisco within the hundred travel days that the trekkers had already announced. For their part, the boys thereafter always cited a praiseworthy new reason for making their arduous journey: they were seeking money with which to pay the cost of college tuition.

The boys' agreement with the company specified that they would skate when and where that was possible, but otherwise they would walk. On June 21, 1910, they reached Chicago, having skated much of the way there. However, from Chicago west—that is, for over two-thirds of the trek's distance—they usually had to walk, being able to skate only through cities and some towns. Although they had already used nearly half of their permitted hundred trekking days, they began to claim that they had 110 days. If so, what a lucky break because, when they arrived in San Francisco on October 4, they had used 107 of those days. Whether or not they got the $2,000 prize, they could at least claim to be the first to attempt to roller-skate across the country. It wasn't their fault that skates don't roll well through mud.

Walking on Water

The wagers taken on by trekkers sometimes had provisions that were both bizarre and daunting; certainly, that was so in 1896 for George J. Mold, a Wichita letter carrier and ventriloquist. To collect $10,000, Mold agreed to stay on the road for four years (traveling by any means), to always wear a clown suit, to return with $20,000 earned along the way, and, during the entire trek, to speak only through a dummy. (He quit after five months, claiming that the continued use of ventriloquism was ruining his voice.) Also demanding were treks specifying novel kinds of locomotion, such as walking backward or on stilts (see chapter 5 again). A standout in this line was Charles W. Oldrieve's astonishing walk on water from Cincinnati to New Orleans done in 1907 on the Ohio and Mississippi Rivers.

Oldrieve began his working life as a high-wire performer, but after his circus employer folded in 1888, he turned his attention full-time to figuring out how to walk on water; that goal had been an obsession ever since he observed water spiders scooting across a pond. Oldrieve's small physique—he was five feet two and weighed 135 pounds—certainly helped his prospects of success. Starting with very wide water shoes that were also more than five feet long, he eventually got their size down to a length of three feet six inches and a width of six inches. Soon, too, he had solved the problems of steering and preventing drag and had perfected a skater's stride (six inches in depth, his shoes remained in the water). Although only nineteen years old, he felt entitled to call himself "professor," a title that stuck. In November of 1888, Professor Oldrieve came to widespread notice by taking up a $500 wager that he could walk down the Hudson River from Albany to New York City within six days. He succeeded, after which came more wagers and walks on water.

Eventually concluding that well-advertised performances were a better way than wager-walks to cash in on his new skill, Oldrieve hired a manager, acquired a new expertise as a pyrotechnist, and developed a repertoire of performances involving explosions and walks on water. A notice in the *Savannah Morning News* on April 20, 1895, for instance, described his colorful "exhibition of a fort attacked by war ships," as follows: "The powder magazine of the fort explodes during the engagement. Prof. Oldrieve in the guise of a modern scientific marine fighter

Capt. Oldrieve Walking on the Water from Cincinnati to New Orleans. 1,800 Miles, on a Wager of $5,000— Passing Helena, Ark., January 25, '07.

As his postcard indicates, while on his rugged water trek Charles Oldrieve upgraded his self-bestowed title from professor to captain.

will walk out upon the water armed with a torpedo gun, with which he will destroy the ship. An exhibition of marine fireworks, sea serpents and other novel combinations will follow."

In 1907, nineteen years after astonishing the world by walking down the Hudson River, Oldrieve took on, in connection with a $5,000 wager, the bigger challenge of walking on the Ohio and Mississippi Rivers from Cincinnati to New Orleans. Departing on January 1, he faced a tight schedule; to cover 1,800 miles within the allotted forty days necessitated averaging 45 miles a day, and at his usual rate of 4 miles an hour, that meant putting in at least eleven hours of very strenuous effort every day. His wife, who was six feet tall, weighed 250 pounds, and claimed to be the world's champion oarswoman, accompanied him in a rowboat, serving as pacemaker, bodyguard, and cheerleader, and once she probably saved his life when he flipped into the river and couldn't get free of his boat-like shoes. Crowds of immense size lining the riverbanks—for instance, an estimated 10,000 persons at Jeffersonville, Indiana—urged him on. Although he ran behind schedule for much of the trip, Oldrieve managed to catch up—he completed his journey on February 10 with forty-five minutes to spare.

Bolstered by his success and celebrity, Oldrieve announced some big plans: after regaining the fifteen pounds he had lost on his river walk, he would take on a $10,000 challenge to walk across the English Channel and follow that up with a walk across the Atlantic Ocean! Those plans were suddenly knocked down, however, by a rapid succession of setbacks, starting with injuries sustained by his wife on July 4 caused by the premature explosion of fireworks connected to one of his routines. Assured that the injuries were not life-threatening, he left to arrange a performance in another city, but he found upon his return several days later that his wife had died. Gripped by grief, he took to heavy drinking. A bartender interrupted his attempt to end his life by drinking chloroform, but Oldrieve succeeded on his second try. So soon after giving his greatest walking performance, the professor had come to the end of his journey.

CHAPTER 2

Why Trek? Attractions and Challenges

A S THE NUMBERS OF PERSONS claiming to be walking on wagers mounted, so, too, did the skepticism that they met along the way. Perhaps hoping to encourage a more welcoming reception, some trekkers made a point of announcing that *they* were not walking on a wager, instead citing loftier or at least more plausible reasons for their treks. In fact, most trekkers, including even some wager-walkers, claimed several motives. Of the various reasons cited beyond walking on a wager or for a prize, four were especially favored—namely, to satisfy a yen for adventure and exploration, to get an up-close look at America, to set a record, and to regain good health.

Trekkers seeking adventure or claiming a zest for exploration covered a wide spectrum, at one end of which were the many whose expressed objective was so vaguely or generally formulated that it could be boiled down to, as several stated, trekking "for the fun of it." Coming under this heading, for instance, were the many members of fraternal lodges who walked to their organizations' national conventions. Included here, too, were the trekkers hoping to break free from the routines of their everyday lives. A surprising number of these were young women trekking in groups of two or three. As one of them informed a reporter for the *Omaha Daily Bee* on May 10, 1915, "we are tired of office work and want to get out to the open road and see something of the country."

At the other end of the spectrum were trekkers who declared that their objective was to learn more about their native land. Although this claim was rarely accompanied by any evidence of systematic inquiry, in a few instances long-haul trekking was clearly used to see and learn more about America and its people. Conducting such a serious investigation was, in fact, as venerable a purpose for trekking as was walking on a wager; in 1867, the year in which Weston introduced long-distance wager-walking, Seth Wilbur Payne took off on a trek from New York to San Francisco for the declared purpose of learning more about the United States. For that same stated reason, the very next year Stephen Powers, following a different route, also trekked from the Atlantic coast to San Francisco, and in 1884 Charles Lummis went from Cincinnati to Los Angeles.

Payne, Powers, and Lummis, as noted in the pages ahead, made strenuous efforts to encounter new sights and experiences along the way, although in doing so they sometimes exposed themselves to considerable danger. Prior to starting the trek, each had also announced his intention to write a book describing his experiences and findings. Although Payne never got around to doing this, he sent thirty-seven dispatches to a Utica newspaper that even today make excellent reading and indicate how seriously he was committed to learning by trekking. Both Powers and Lummis did carry out their pledges to publish books.

Although these three men clearly lived up to a notion of the trekker as adventurous inquirer and serious student, that was not so for others making the same claims who followed them. "I'll write a book!" did become a familiar mantra for many trekkers, but most of those books were never written.

Another stated purpose for trekking was to set a time record. This objective was easy to assert because trekking had no established categories of competition or official registries of records. It was no surprise, then, that many trekkers claimed that they were pursuing a record of one kind or another—or, indeed, that they already held world records in their chosen competitive categories.

Striving for a record-breaking performance received a new stimulus and competitive format after Weston returned to cross-country trekking in 1907. Now the stated objective for aspiring champions could be formulated as outperforming America's most famous competitive walker; particularly favored targets for challenge were Weston's performances in his walk in 1909 from New York to San Francisco and in his trek in 1913 from New York to Minneapolis. Setting a trekking record was soon subsumed under a new heading: beating Weston's time, something many trekkers announced that they aimed to do.

Regaining good health was a fourth favored justification for making long-distance treks; in fact, probably only walking to win a wager or a prize was cited more often as a reason. Gravely ill and wasting away, so the story often went, the trekker learned from a doctor that he or she suffered from tuberculosis or another serious illness and that taking long walks in the open air and sunshine offered the only hope of relief. Adopting long-distance trekking on a doctor's orders, the patient found that the treatment brought salubrious results. But how valid were those diagnoses? And would any doctor ever really prescribe a 3,400-mile trek? That many trekkers would push this line is easy to understand, however; nicely honed to elicit the sympathies of listeners, it also lay beyond easy challenge by scoffers. Newspaper reports reveal that the long-distance "walking cure" was touted by trekkers to treat other maladies, too, including "paralysis" (no further explanation provided), obesity, and the general run-down condition then called malaise. Two veterans of World War I gassed in fighting in France asserted in the *Gettysburg (PA) Star and Sentinel* on November 19, 1921, that a trek from New York to Los Angeles helped them, as they put it, "get the gas out of their systems."

Brief accounts follow of some of the trekkers who set out on long journeys on foot to get a close look at America, find adventure, beat Weston's time, or regain good health. Like many other trekkers, they sometimes cited more than one reason for their jaunts.

"A Poor Student"

Sometime early in 1867, Seth Wilbur Payne, a twenty-nine-year-old resident of Utica, New York, set sail from New York to Glasgow, there to begin a walking tour of the British Isles and Western Europe. Although information about his earlier years is scanty, he likely had already done brief stints as a college student, a schoolteacher, a newspaper reporter, and even a newspaper publisher and editor. Working most recently as a farmhand, he had somehow managed to save enough money not only to pay for his ocean passage but also to have $300 left to cover expenses while walking in Europe.

Payne's plan took a big hit when a pickpocket in Glasgow nabbed his purse and with it his $300. He stuck to his plan, however, occasionally taking time off to work as he traveled and spending his meager earnings very carefully (he calculated his daily expenses at fourteen cents). His penurious circumstances brought him into close contact with many poor working-class persons ("slaves of the aristocracy," in his judgment), for whom he developed much admiration and sympathy. From them he got "hundreds of smart questions about America" that he was unable to answer and that "taught me how little I really knew of my own country. In fact, in many instances I was looked upon as an imposter, so [great] was my ignorance," the *Utica Weekly Herald* reported on November 16, 1867. Eventually came a change of plan: after completing his tour of the British Isles, Payne decided, he would come home and take a walking tour of the United States. The rest of the world could wait until he had learned more about his own country and its people.

Once back in New York, Payne completed plans for his trek, which he would finance by working and lecturing along the way. He also arranged to send letters to the *Utica Weekly Herald* as he traveled. Ultimately, Payne produced thirty-seven letters that were published in the Utica newspaper under the heading "From the Atlantic to the Pacific on Foot" and that carried his byline of "A Poor Student."

When Payne began his long walk on November 11, 1867, newspapers hailed him as a "Weston rival" in pursuit of "the second great pedestrian feat." Payne stressed, however, that he was not walking to win a wager or to set a time record but, rather, to advance his knowledge of America. In his fifth letter, published in *Utica Weekly Herald* of December 24, 1867,

The *Philadelphia Inquirer* was not the only newspaper to wonder why Seth Wilbur Payne was making his unprecedented cross-country trek.

he noted that "I make a practice on entering a town of any size to seek lodging at a private boarding house, where I am less annoyed by the curious [and] have an opportunity to learn more of the social nature of the people." Here was a sharp contrast with the playing to "the curious" indulged in by Weston and most other trekkers in years to come.

Following a trail west across Pennsylvania, Payne at Pittsburgh headed southwest for Cincinnati and from there pushed on to Indianapolis, Springfield, St. Louis, and Kansas City. Reaching St. Joseph during a blizzard on February 15, he decided to haul up until spring and spent the next two months visiting many midwestern cities by train. On April 23, 1868, he resumed his trek, following the Union Pacific Railroad's trackage, still under construction, from Omaha to Utah along the forthcoming transcontinental rail route. For protection against attacks by Sioux and Cheyenne warriors, he traveled with others nearly to Salt Lake City, but thereafter he walked alone, including across the desert and the Sierra Nevadas. On July 30, 1868, he was in San Francisco, where he booked his steamship passage to Panama and, after crossing the isthmus, on to New York.

Payne clearly was "A Poor Student" only in a pecuniary, not a pedagogical, sense. His letters are well written and disclose an inquiring mind eager to get the most out of his unusual trip. Found there are informative and often entertaining accounts of, for instance, his discovery of a well-stocked library in Cincinnati; a horse auction in Kansas City; conversations with Lincoln's law partner William Herndon, Brigham Young, and miscellaneous farmers and mechanics; an overnight stay in a Pawnee village; Cheyenne's many debauched features; and the rise and fall of other railroad boom towns. He went on to a career in journalism, which was cut short, however, by his death from pneumonia at the age of forty-three. Regrettably, he never wrote the trek account that he had intended, but his letters would be well worth retrieving and publishing. Doing so would also give a more secure and fitting recognition to the first person who believed that a walk across the entirety of America made sense and then proceeded to do it.

Another Route to Frisco

On January 1, 1868, only fifty-one days after Payne's departure from New York, Stephen Powers took off from Raleigh, North Carolina, on a trek to San Francisco, arriving there on November 3, about three months after Payne's arrival. For seven months, from January through July, the men were both pushing westward, but a chance meeting of the two trekkers was never a possibility. Traveling well to the south of Payne's route, Powers walked first to Charleston and Savannah before turning west and moving through the Gulf Coast states and the territories of New Mexico and Arizona on his 3,700-mile journey to the Pacific coast.

While on his trek, Powers celebrated his twenty-eighth birthday. During his first eighteen years, he had lived and worked on his father's farm in Ohio, but he left in 1858 to enroll in the "classical curriculum" at the University of Michigan. After graduating in 1863 with a bachelor's degree, he was hired as a reporter for the *Cincinnati Commercial*, assigned to cover such major events of the Civil War as the Battle of Kennesaw Mountain, Sherman's campaign in Georgia, and Lincoln's funeral. After the war, he traveled throughout the South to report on Reconstruction activities, and in 1866 he testified in the U.S. House of Representatives on the progress of Reconstruction, especially on the work of the Freedmen's Bureau. Later that year, he began a fifteen-month stint as a correspondent in Germany covering the Austro-Prussian War for the *New York Times* and several other publications.

Before returning to the United States near the end of 1867, Powers took several walking tours of Germany and Switzerland, which perhaps gave him the notion of trekking across the American continent. There is no evidence that he had ever heard of Weston, Payne, and their treks. Unlike them, he did not publicize his trekking intentions beyond informing some close friends and family members, who tried to dissuade him. The complete absence of a newspaper trail for his trek indicates that he also made no effort to alert the press as he moved west. What is known about his trek comes from his own 327-page account, *Afoot and Alone: A Walk from Sea to Sea by the Southern Route*, published in 1872. There he indicated that his trek was "undertaken, partly, from a love of wild adventure [and] partly from a wish to make personal and ocular study

CAPTURED.

Coming upon menacing Apache braves, Stephen Powers successfully met the danger
by posing as a harmless simpleton, as illustrated in this engraving from his book.

of the most diverse races of the Republic." These purposes, of course,
were similar to Payne's.

Held alongside Payne's engaging dispatches, however, Powers's book
greatly disappoints. His descriptions of natural scenery and geologi-
cal and meteorological features are often interesting, and he provides
some good sketches of characters and events encountered along the way,
especially his tense meet-up with a band of Apaches. But the results of
his purported "study of the most diverse races" too often are glib and
preposterous generalizations. Examples: "Be just to an Indian, but never
be generous. Generosity they take for weakness." "The Texans have the
reputation of being the laziest people in the U.S., and so they are, with
the exception of the freedmen." "The inferiority of Pacific tribes to the
Eastern Indians" was a result of diet; the latter ate "plenty of good red
meat," but "the Pacific tribes ate principally grasshoppers and grubs."
"The difference between white and black [people] is indicated in the

remark of Themistocles, who said he could not learn to fiddle, but he could make a great city grow where a village was before." This last item points to another huge problem with Powers's book: every several pages, he displays his erudition by inserting historical or literary references not always apt to be known by most readers. Eventually, even Powers concluded that *Afoot and Alone* was a "valueless work."

Fetched by California's charms, Powers spent the next six years visiting the state's Indian tribes on foot and writing articles about them. Eventually these articles were collected and published by the U.S. Department of the Interior, indicating, surely, that his ethnological prowess and writing style had greatly improved. Returning to the family farm in Ohio, he next took up breeding sheep and writing fiction but failed at the latter. At his death in 1904, he was in Florida growing oranges and strawberries and editing the *Florida Farmer and Fruit Grower.*

A Tramp across the Continent

Charles Fletcher Lummis was a bright but not very attentive student at Harvard University, where he was a member of the class of 1881 (one year behind his good friend Teddy Roosevelt). Devoting his undergraduate years mainly to playing sports and poker, socializing, and writing poetry, he was often in trouble with the university authorities. Not bothering to show up for several exams in the final semester of his senior year, he let a Harvard diploma slip away. Lummis nonetheless still hung around Cambridge, disclosing at last that in his junior year he had secretly married a Boston University medical student and awaited her graduation before taking any next steps. Meanwhile, he wrote poetry and earned a meager income by tutoring students at Harvard and other nearby institutions.

In 1882, Lummis accepted his father-in-law's proposal that he manage the family's 600-acre farm near Chillicothe, Ohio. Before that year was over, however, he had moved on to become the editor and sole reporter of a Chillicothe weekly newspaper, the *Scioto Gazette.* His editorials soon got noticed, and that led to a correspondence with the editor of the *Los Angeles Times*, whom Lummis eventually asked for a job. In hiring Lummis, the editor also agreed to the young man's proposal to walk to his new job in Los Angeles and send in weekly dispatches along the way. After making similar arrangements ($5 per weekly letter) with the *Chillicothe Leader*, mapping a route, deciding on trekking apparel, and sending his wife ahead by train, Lummis departed from Cincinnati on September 12, 1884.

In *A Tramp across the Continent*, published in 1892, Lummis explained why he made that trek, starting with a confession virtually identical to the one made earlier by Seth Wilbur Payne: "I am an American and felt ashamed to know so little of my own country as I did, and as most Americans do." His trek, he reasoned, would provide the opportunity "to learn more of the country and its people than railroad travel could ever teach." As his book discloses, the gregarious Lummis regularly sought out the company of the railroad workers, cowboys, and many others he met on the way. Singing with them and learning new songs were among his special joys.

Because Lummis's trek was made more than a decade and a half after those of Payne and Powers, the challenges he faced were in some respects

As his publicity photo reveals, Charles Lummis dressed oddly for a cross-country trek—none-too-roomy knickers, tight knee-high stockings (they were bright red!), and conventional street shoes. Photo courtesy of the Autry Museum of the American West, P. 32526.

less daunting. Routing his trek along rail lines, he could ship luggage and equipment ahead by train, and he ate many meals and slept many nights in railroad section houses. However, he often made side excursions to hunt and explore, which added many hundreds of miles and more risks to his trek. In one instance he faced real peril: falling twenty feet when a ledge gave way, Lummis landed on his left forearm, breaking it and puncturing the skin. His account of realigning the bone and treating the wound makes for fascinating but discomfiting reading.

In Denver, Lummis learned of snowstorms in Utah and decided to turn south. That proved to be a decision of eye-opening and even life-changing consequence, for he soon fell in love with New Mexico. In his book, he also details encounters he had there with Mexicans, Native Americans, and Spanish Americans that led him to jettison prejudices he had harbored against those peoples. By the time he reached Los Angeles on February 1, 1885, Lummis had indeed achieved his goal of learning much about America.

After losing his job with the *Los Angeles Times* in 1887, Lummis returned to New Mexico, but by 1892 Los Angeles was again his hometown, this time for the rest of his life. There he edited *Out West*, a magazine of regional history and culture, wrote many books and articles about the Southwest and its peoples, and championed Native Americans in their struggles with the U.S. Bureau of Indian Affairs. Furthermore, as head librarian of the Los Angeles Public Library from 1905 to 1910, he greatly strengthened that institution both as a public library and as a research facility.

Although studded with many solid achievements, Lummis's life also had a bohemian tinge first seen in his years at Harvard and his "tramp across the continent" and reflected in the frequent parties he hosted and his continuing peculiarities of hairstyling and clothing. His second wife found further evidence of an offbeat lifestyle when she discovered, in Lummis's diary, accounts of about fifty extramarital affairs.

The Arizona Limited

Michael Garber Harman practiced law in Virginia, but on February 8, 1904, he left San Francisco on a trek that would take him first to Los Angeles and then on to New York City. Harman seems to fit much of the pattern set earlier by Seth Wilbur Payne, Stephen Powers, and Charles Fletcher Lummis. Like them, he was in his twenties, smart, and well educated. Like them, too, he planned to write about his trek and did follow through with *The Arizona Limited; or, Across the Continent Afoot*, published in 1909. Finally, just as those predecessors had done, he claimed an educational purpose for his long trek, noting in his book his excited contemplation of "how much of God's country [I] will be enabled to see and study."

Unlike those three earlier trekkers, however, Harman directed much time and effort to seeking the limelight and scrounging for financial support. To begin his trek, he hired a four-piece fife and drum corps to precede him for a mile and a half down a main street in San Francisco; then, after speaking briefly, he peddled fifteen photos of himself at ten cents each. Included in the procession was a burro bearing a sign advertising a horse and mule sale; for this Harman received $7. Seeking financing in imaginative ways was necessitated by another well-advertised feature of his trek: he would start with only three cents in his pocket.

Coming down with the flu one day after starting his trek, Harman hauled up in Palo Alto, and for the next five days he obtained free room and board from the members of the Stanford University chapter of his college fraternity. His forward movement was next interrupted by a four-week stay in Los Angeles (how he paid for it is not known), but by early May he had reached Albuquerque. There he met a man named Tim, with whom, from pieces of found junk, he constructed a four-wheeled vehicle, which he christened the Arizona Limited Express. After swapping some of their tools for four burros, the partners were on their attention-getting way to St. Louis. There for several months they found various ways to take in money at that city's world's fair. After having a falling-out with Tim, Harman trudged on with a new partner named Heine, arriving in New York on December 15.

Especially in its earliest pages, Harman's narrative recounts some interesting experiences—for instance, finding odd characters in the

ARRIVED AT INDIANAPOLIS.

Michael Harman, Heine, and their burro companions made a big hit when, as depicted in this photo from Harman's book, the Arizona Limited arrived in Indianapolis.

desert, encountering menacing tramps, and dodging a train on a high trestle. After Albuquerque, however, too much of his book centers on the frequent breakdowns and patchwork repairs of the Arizona Limited and accounts of the burros and their tendency to go astray. Particularly cloying are the cutesy names (for instance, Mark Twain and Carrie Nation) that Harman bestowed on the burros and the frequent insights, comments, and soliloquies that he attributes to them.

In his next-to-last chapter, Harman asks, "Is traveling on three cents an easy proposition?" Answering in the negative, of course, he notes that a trekker "must be tactful, versatile to a degree, an adept in the art of flattering, have what is vulgarly termed 'unlimited nerve,' and be able to measure off chin-music by the yard." He delights in recounting many examples of smooth-talking hotel and restaurant managers, toll collectors, farmers, and others to meet his and his burros' needs gratis. His dexterous practice of these skills, he acknowledges, would constitute "graft" if nothing of equal value was given in exchange. Presumably, however, he met that requirement by offering entertainment.

Harman's purpose in trekking had clearly shifted from his original stated intent, one often expressed by trekkers, of learning about "God's country." His true goals, it turns out, were to have fun, put on a good show, and see what he could get away with.

Girl Hikers Headed West

Surely no other trekker had the chutzpah of Michael Harman, but some did share his sense of gratification in meeting the challenges of a long trek. Once those trekkers had tired of making half-hearted or implausible claims about restoring health, setting a record, or learning about America, they usually confessed their true purpose very simply: trekking for pleasure. Two such pleasure seekers were Frances Leach, age twenty-three, and Mary Coyne, age eighteen, who together walked from Denver to San Francisco in 1913.

Leach and Coyne were employed as shopgirls in a Denver department store, where, in spite of their youth and brief experience, they had already become work-weary. Customers were so "insulting," and their health was starting to "fail" under the daily grind. Fortunately, however, they discovered long-haul trekking and took it up as a "pastime and recreation," as they told one reporter. Deciding that they would trek to San Francisco, they told another reporter that they were "making the trip for no other purpose than pleasure and experience." But the trek did have salubrious consequences for their health, too; after only four weeks, both reported feeling much stronger, and each was delighted to have gained (!) fifteen pounds.

By no means was their trek an easy one. They left Denver on May 17 but found the snow at Berthoud Pass still so deep that they needed two tries to get across the Continental Divide. They followed the Midland Trail, an old wagon trail then being developed for automobile use, to Salt Lake City but found that there was no road at many places. Although they reported receiving kind treatment from most of the people they encountered on the way, on two occasions they were menaced by tramps and had to drive them off by firing warning shots from the pistols they carried.

On several nights, Leach and Coyne slept in railroad section houses (keeping their pistols at hand), but usually they were accommodated in hotels or farmhouses along the way. Because they carried no change of clothes, sometimes they spent the day in bed while their garments were sent out to be washed. They met their expenses mainly by selling postcards showing them in their trekking regalia, but in Salt Lake City they also earned money working as street vendors selling newspapers and magazines.

FRANCES LEACH   MARY COYNE
Walking from Denver to San Francisco

The postcard sold by Frances Leach and Mary Coyne depicts two
young women finding fame and happiness as the girl hikers.

Leach and Coyne left Salt Lake City on the old Oregon Trail, intending to go to San Francisco by way of Portland. In Pocatello, Idaho, however, they met up with Leach's cousin, Bert Adams, and, accompanied by him, turned south after reaching Twin Falls. Presumably, Adams convinced them to cash in on their celebrity as the girl hikers, because thereafter newspaper accounts indicated that they became vaudeville performers offering both a musical act and an exhibition of boxing, and those accounts also identified Adams as their manager. Doubtless under his influence, too, they began to talk about continuing their trek to Florida and then on to Europe.

When the three trekkers reached San Francisco on August 17, Leach and Coyne had been traveling for three months, covering about 1,900 miles at an average of nearly 25 miles per walking day. (On one day, they achieved 72 miles, spurred on by the paucity of water in their canteens.) After resting for three days, the trio took off for Los Angeles and then turned east. Possibly Adams's long-range plan was to go on to Florida, but his first goal was to reach New Orleans within seventy-five days. As for the girl hikers, they were ready to end their trek. Once they reached Galveston, they planned to head north and return to Denver. Whether that also meant a return to those dreadful department store jobs is not known.

Trekking for the "Fun of the Thing"

On May 15, 1913, Kerr Forman and Waldo Wallis, young commercial artists living in Kansas City, set out on a trek to Montreal, billing themselves as the Vagabond Artists. They told a reporter that they hoped for improvement in their physical condition, claiming, like Frances Leach and Mary Coyne, that their health had been "undermined" by "close application to work" done for too long "inside a building." Finding that claim implausible, however, the reporter observed in the *Keytesville (MO) Chariton Courier* of May 23, 1913, that "the boys did not look like people who were suffering invalidism, and the prank looks more like a trip [done] for the novelty of the thing than anything else." Another reporter concluded, too, that there was "nothing of the vagabond in their appearance." The reporters' suspicions were justified. Forman and Wallis were simply taking a break from their usual routines and even acknowledged at other moments that their trek was being done mostly "just for the fun of the thing."

That fun consisted of walking about fifteen miles a day and camping each night along the road or in a public park. The two also sketched or painted scenes observed on the way and then sold these artworks, as well as postcards depicting themselves, to get the money needed to finance the trek. They carried their tent, cooking equipment, food, dining utensils, and art supplies in a two-wheeled box cart pulled by a pony. Because two folding chairs were also on board, and the end of the cart came down to serve as a table, the men were also able to dine graciously as they traveled.

The Vagabond Artists expected to reach Montreal about September 1. Did they get there? That is not known, but on August 14 a newspaper reported that they had been spotted in London, Ontario.

In 1916, another young man, George Demers, felt the same wanderlust that had bestirred Forman and Wallis to embark on a long trek purely for enjoyment. Demers was then twenty-six years old and living in San Francisco, where he earned a meager income performing as a stage magician. Deciding to move back to his hometown of Lowell, Massachusetts, he hit upon the idea of making the trip by walking. In fine physical shape, he explicitly rejected making any claim about trekking to improve his health. To one reporter he confessed that he was making the trek "for

KERR FORMAN AND WALDO WALLIS
The "Vagabond Artists" who are
Walking from Kansas City to Montreal

As they advanced, the self-proclaimed Vagabond Artists financed their trek by selling their artworks and these postcards.

The "Vagabond Artists" in Camp During their Walk from Kansas City to Montreal

the sport there is in it," but then he found a grander reason: he could try to set a record. His announced goal was to walk to Lowell in fewer than the 105 days Weston had taken to go from New York to San Francisco in 1909. Demers took off on February 28.

The absurdity of Demers's quest was very quickly evident. Unlike Weston, Demers had to invest time as he traveled in earning money to meet his expenses. In addition to performing in small-town theaters as Demers, the Hobo Magician, he did many odd jobs for farmers. And, again unlike Weston, Demers pulled a cart, which weighed 115 pounds when filled and more when carrying water. The cart was designed to accommodate cooking, eating, and sleeping but frequently was disabled by tire and wheel problems. Facing deep snow in the Sierra Nevadas, Demers twice had to put the cart on a train and then await its delivery at stops farther ahead.

Soon abandoning the idea of outperforming Weston, Demers came up with another notion. Since most of his trek would be done on the Lincoln Highway, why not get the Lincoln Highway Association to hire him to make reports about the road's condition? When the association declined to do so, he made detailed reports anyway. He had found his trek's true purpose.

On September 15, Demers arrived in Lowell, 200 days after his departure. Regrettably, no photo of him and his "electric-lighted hotel on wheels" has yet come to light.

Breaking Weston's Record

Demers's assault on Weston's 1909 transcontinental trek record was so ill planned that it's hard to believe he took the project seriously. Perhaps that was so, too, for others who declared their intent to beat Weston's record but were never heard from again. A fast-paced trek across the United States was, after all, a difficult undertaking. Because much planning, training, dedication, and perseverance were required, most of the attempts to dislodge Weston from his championship would likely fail.

Several challenges did succeed, however—for instance, the effort made by John Henry Mooney in 1911. Mooney, a firefighter in New York City, proposed to walk from there to San Francisco in eighty-five days, thereby beating Weston's 1909 record by twenty days. Pledging $1 each, Mooney's fellow firefighters throughout the city allegedly raised $10,000 that would be his if he met his objective. Doubtless spurred on by the prospect of bringing in such a large prize, Mooney finished his trek in eighty-one days, as reported in the *San Francisco Call* on September 6, 1911.

Also soon breaking Weston's 1909 record was Henry W. Shelton, identified in a newspaper article as a "licensed public porter" working in New York City. Although he had lived in the United States for thirty-five years, Shelton was born and lived his first two decades in Cuba, and thus for trekking purposes he felt entitled to claim the sobriquet of the Cuban Wonder. By 1915, he had gained much experience as a pedestrian competitor, claiming in an article published in the *Fort Wayne (IN) Journal Gazette* on September 2, 1915, that "in St. Louis I broke the records when I walked for 100 continuous hours. The first 50 miles I walked in six hours and eighteen minutes, and in Madison Square Garden . . . I walked 766 miles and one lap in a week. In St. Louis I walked 412 miles in eighty-eight hours." Now he was ready to take on Weston's time in trekking from New York to San Francisco. Several weeks before departing, Shelton attended a party held in celebration of Weston's seventy-sixth birthday. On that happy occasion, Shelton disclosed, the old trekker graciously passed on to his fifty-four-year-old challenger some "pointers on the art of pedestrianism."

Shelton left New York on April 1, 1915, and arrived in San Francisco on June 23, taking a total of eighty-one walking days for the trek. On July 15, he set off on a return trek to New York, which took, by his report,

HENRY W. SHELTON

"The Cuban Wonder"

CHAMPION LONG DISTANCE WALKER OF THE WORLD

Under Auspices of the

New York News

IS WALKING FROM NEW YORK TO LE GRAND
AND RETURN---2414 MILES---IN 60 DAYS.

Left
NewYork **JUNE 3, AT NOON**

Arrived
LeGrand **JUNE 30.**

Mr. Shelton announces that on Saturday Evening, at 7 o'clock, he will give a free exhibition of heel and toe walking at the Public Square, after which he will make a talk from the band stand, relating some of his experiences on his record trip from New York to San Francisco and return, covering 7000 miles en route.

Readers of the *Le Grand Reporter* learned on June 30, 1916, the exciting news that Henry Shelton had reached their town on his great trek from New York.

only seventy walking days. In sum, on his round trip he covered 6,768 miles in 151 days for an average performance of nearly 45 miles per day. These results, if true, were astounding. To achieve them, Shelton said he had walked thirteen to fifteen hours nearly every day of the trek and often walked far into the night.

The next year, Shelton promoted another big trekking project, this one having the sponsorship of the *New York Daily News*: he would walk from New York to Le Grand, Iowa, and back—a total of 2,414 miles—in a maximum of sixty days, averaging 40 miles or more per day. Why Le Grand was chosen as the trek's western terminus remains a mystery. However, this small town in central Iowa had the good fortune of being on the Lincoln Highway, which was Shelton's route in his two transcontinental treks in 1915. Perhaps on his two passes through Le Grand he had been especially warmly received. Certainly, on both occasions the local newspaper gave him long and favorable coverage.

Shelton did each half of his 1916 trek from New York to Le Grand and back in twenty-eight days. More than one hundred years later, his total of fifty-six days for the round trip still stands as the record. Indeed, the Cuban Wonder seems likely to hold that record forever.

Pestering Weston

After completing an impressive seventy-five-day walk from Los Angeles to New York in 1910, Weston declared it to be his last long trek. But old habits are hard to break, and in 1913, at age seventy-four, he contracted to take a leisurely walk of sixty days from New York to Minneapolis during June and July. On his way, he encountered many admiring crowds—but also some annoying noises made by an upstart trekker, Samuel A. Debs.

Debs was often identified in the press as a "newspaper man," but that was so only in the sense that he sold newspapers at a stand in New York City and was active in the newspaper carriers union. In 1912–13, he claimed to have trekked from New York to San Francisco to "study labor conditions." On his return trip to New York, he proposed to break Weston's transcontinental record, but that trek appears not to have happened. Then, in early June of 1913, he learned that Weston was already one week into his trek from New York to Minneapolis. He saw a splendid opportunity: despite Weston's one-week head start, Debs could take him on and not only pull ahead and win but set a record time for the trek between the two cities.

Debs took off on June 9, passed Weston in eastern Indiana in the first week of July, and reached Minneapolis on July 20, beating Weston's time by twenty days. But there was no genuine contest: Weston was under contract to follow a tightly regulated sixty-day schedule, arriving on August 2 to lay the cornerstone of the Minneapolis Athletic Club's new quarters. Because newspaper coverage carried Debs's false claim of a contest (one that had Weston losing badly, moreover), Weston became increasingly enraged. Finally, he struck back: railroad workers had told him, he said, that Debs was seen riding on freight trains, and policemen in Chicago had reported seeing him riding on an elevated train across that city. But what the true facts were no longer mattered. With the press's help, Debs had succeeded in constructing a bogus claim that he cited many times thereafter—namely, that he had decisively defeated Weston in the great New York–to–Minneapolis trekking contest of 1913.

Also making unwarranted use of Weston's 1913 trek as a fair target for competitive challenge was Marie Chester of Middletown, New York, who left New York for Minneapolis on August 1, just as Weston was arriving in that city. Likely a widow, this forty-nine-year-old woman supported herself, her ten children, and her "aged father," all of whom lived with

MRS. M. B. CHESTER AND CHILDREN on Walking Tour
from New York City to Minneapolis—1913

Marie Chester's fifteen-year-old daughter joined Marie and two of her
sons on their long trek too late to be included on their postcard.

her, by working as a seamstress. However, in February, fire destroyed her house and severely affected her health, particularly her eyesight. Having to quit work, she began taking frequent long walks to regain her strength. When she learned of Weston's trek, she was certain she could beat his projected sixty days, and some friends urged her to give it a try. That notion took firm hold after other friends pledged to give her $2,000 toward rebuilding her house if she could match or beat Weston's time.

Departing from New York with two sons, ages thirteen and fourteen, Chester was soon joined by her fifteen-year-old daughter. The four camped every night on their trek, which followed Weston's route along the tracks of the Erie and the Chicago and North Western Railroads. A Newfoundland dog pulled a wagon that carried a tent and the postcards they sold along the way to finance their trek. On September 29, sixty days after their departure, they were in Minneapolis, having matched Weston's time (and taking only fifty-three walking days to do so). Happy news soon followed, too, that the trek's sponsors were increasing Chester's prize to $4,000.

Newspapers loved this story, one noting that Weston had some catching up to do to remain the champion walker. Whether Weston felt threatened or merely irked is not known.

Families Trekking for Health

That Marie Chester was accompanied on her trek by three of her children was not surprising or unusual. Many husband-and-wife teams engaged in long-distance trekking, and sometimes they were accompanied by children, who could range from young adults all the way down to babes in arms. Various reasons were given for these family expeditions, but restoring health—either a parent's or a child's—was one of the most favored. The maladies alleged were often described in the vaguest of terms, such as "failing health" or "a run-down condition," and the treks were usually financed by the sale of postcards. Little is known today about most of these families seeking cures through trekking—for instance, about the Ballard family shown in the postcard on page 109. About those depicted in the two postcards on page 108, however, at least a few facts are available.

Mr. and Mrs. Reuben E. Fenton lived in Schenectady, New York, with their seven children, who ranged in age from five to twenty-three. In 1913, the parents got the unhappy news from a physician that the health of son Gilbert, age eighteen, as well as of two of the other children, was "failing" and that what was needed for their treatment was "out-of-doors life." The Fentons decided to relocate the family to the balmier clime of California and to begin the needed open-air treatment at once by having the family walk to their new home.

On May 1, 1913, the nine Fentons took off on a trek to San Francisco projected to last two years. In the first year they would aim to reach Kansas City, spend the winter there, and conclude the trek the next year. Family belongings were carried in a prairie schooner six feet wide and ten feet long pulled by a horse team. The three oldest boys slept in a tent, but the others slept in the schooner, each side of which bore this inscription: "The Fenton Family / Walking from Schenectady N.Y. to San Francisco California May 1st, 1913. We are dependent on the sale of postcards and books for our living." (What those books were is not known.)

An article published in a Salem, Ohio, newspaper indicates that the Fentons got to that city on August 13, but the lack of further newspaper coverage strongly hints that the family never made it to California. In fact, four years later Gilbert Fenton was still living and working in Schenectady. Featured in a newspaper ad, he reported that his health problems

Sure to elicit sympathy and sales
were postcards depicting entire
families trekking to surmount
health problems.

J. S. Leddy, Wife, Babies, Orlando, Fla. to Southern Ind.

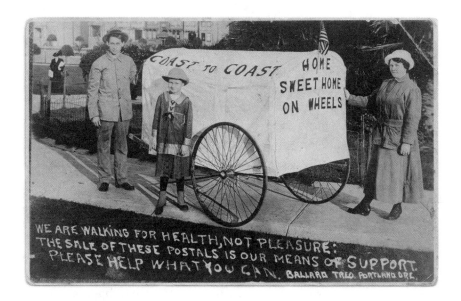

had finally cleared up, not by trekking, however, but rather by his taking Tanlac, a patent medicine.

The Leddy family postcard on page 108 illustrates another variant of a family trekking in pursuit of improved health. For twenty-two years, J. S. Leddy had been a house painter in North Carolina, but in 1915, sustaining permanent injuries from a fall, he gave up that work and moved to Indiana. Undergoing two major operations and suffering from worsening vision, he was advised to go to Florida for his health. Not finding work there, however, and broke, he came back to Indiana on foot in October of 1921, accompanied by his wife and pushing a wheelbarrow carrying a 300-pound load that included their worldly goods; a daughter, age nineteen months; and a son, age two months.

Thus began a new line of activity consisting of at least three more treks of ever-widening range between Indiana and Florida over the next three years. As the family trekked, Leddy earned money by painting names on mailboxes and sharpening scissors but found that selling postcards door to door was more profitable. Soon came an announcement that the family would do a transcontinental trek to improve Leddy's health and to earn enough money to build a house for their retirement. Newspaper accounts ended in late 1924, however. As the children grew, perhaps the wheelbarrow became just too heavy for an invalid to push.

The Walking Woolfs

In the heyday of trekking, probably the best-known advocates of trekking as a means of recovering good health were Dwight H. and Stella Woolf, a young married couple living in Kansas City, where he was a violinist and music publisher and she was a stenographer. Their story began with Dwight spending long days absorbed in his work and neglecting his health. As his weight steadily fell, at last reaching a pitiful 107 pounds, he described himself as becoming a "nervous wreck." Consulting a physician, he got the alarming news that he would die soon if he didn't change his daily routine; above all, he needed to spend more time out of doors exercising in fresh air. At that point, Stella had a great idea: "Let's walk, for I'm going along."

What followed was a 300-mile trek made in the latter half of 1909 through the Ozark Mountains, accompanied by a packhorse and their "faithful dog, Don." Exhausted after walking six miles on the first day, Dwight nonetheless stuck with the program and soon saw great improvement in his strength. By the end of their walk through the Ozarks, his health was obviously improving rapidly, and he was now an enthusiastic trekker, eager to take on an excursion to New York City in 1910. During the next four years after that trek, they covered every part of the United States in three more jaunts made entirely on foot. Eventually, Dwight's weight climbed to 144 pounds (and Stella's fell from 194 to 170 pounds). Now known as the Walking Woolfs, they were enthusiastically received everywhere by large crowds, public officials, and such celebrities as Douglas Fairbanks, William Jennings Bryan, and Teddy Roosevelt.

The Woolfs walked fifteen to twenty-five miles a day and, except when in major cities, prepared their own meals and camped out every night. They were accompanied on all treks by their loyal canine companion, Don, and on every trek except the first one by their horse, Dolley, who pulled a two-wheeled cart carrying their luggage, tent, food, and supplies. Among those supplies were photography equipment, a violin, large quantities of Walking Woolfs postcards, and a big supply of song sheets for "Take a Walk," a tune composed by Dwight. As they traveled, Stella took elaborate notes, from which came a co-authored book, *Tramping and Camping*, published in 1912 following the completion of their third trek. Thereafter, poor Dolley's burdens were increased by the weight

Mr. and Mrs. D. H. WOOLF, their horse Dolley, and their faithful dog, Don. Walking down Broadway, New York City, August 15th. Started from Kansas City, Monday, May 2nd, 1910

Our song "TAKE "A WALK" has no equal

MR. and MRS. D. H. WOOLF starting on their long walk, half way around the U. S., Saturday, Oct. 15, 1910

Among the several dozen postcards issued by the Walking Woolfs were these depicting their arrival in New York on August 15, 1910, and their departure for the West Coast two months later.

of these books, which, like postcards and song sheets, the Woolfs sold to raise the funds used to finance their treks. Other sources of income were lectures, slideshows, and stunt violin performances, all presented in movie theaters.

Dwight was fond of citing an apothegm of his own concoction: "When you get into a rut, walk out of it." Perhaps sensing that trekking had itself become a rut, however, he and Stella gave it up in 1915. By then, he had long since regained his health, and they had made two treks across the United States, walked up and down both coasts and throughout the Midwest, and had compiled a total of 25,000 miles of walking. Still dedicated to promoting walking as the best medicine (and to keeping alive the public's memory of their achievements), they stayed on the move but did so now by traveling in a red Ford automobile bearing "The Walking Woolfs" painted on its sides and carrying a huge archive of photos, slides, and a movie documenting their treks.

By 1919, they were on their third transcontinental run by automobile. An article published in the *Columbia Evening Missourian* on May 17 of that year recounted their usual procedure: "They rent a movie house, put on their pictures, and by the aid of a calliope attachment in the car, Mr. Woolf plays a dozen or more tunes. A crowd quickly gathers and the show is on. Mrs. Woolf lectures, telling of their personal experiences in connection with each picture." It is not known when the Woolfs made their final presentation of this charming show.

Gals, Guns, and Tuberculosis

Although Dwight Woolf attributed his run-down condition and severe weight loss to "nervous exhaustion," other trekkers having those symptoms believed they pointed to tuberculosis (or consumption, as it was often called then). The doctors' orders were always the same: get lots of outdoor exercise. (Here's a question: were these diagnoses and this prescription really made by physicians?) The afflicted ones usually claimed to find quick relief, even a cure, in trekking. That was the case for each of the following three young women.

On January 11, 1915, a sickly nineteen-year-old Phyllis Skrehot set out from Denver to walk along the long "southern route" to San Francisco, hoping to improve her health. Accompanied by a burro pulling a wagon, Skrehot was in Los Angeles by April 28. There an Associated Press article highlighted the significance of her trek: although she had started as a patient "whom the doctors gave up last January as a hopeless victim of tuberculosis," she now, by her report at least, "enjoyed perfect health." Moreover, in less than four months of trekking, she had put on 30 healthy pounds and now tipped the scale at 125 pounds.

As Skrehot neared San Francisco, she appears to have become increasingly ebullient, perhaps even frisky. When she accidentally shot a man in the forearm in San Juan Bautista, the local *Morning Tribune* on July 1, 1915, declared her to be "the modern type of femininity" and recommended that "mere man . . . make himself scarce" when encountering her on the highway. After resting for two months in San Francisco, she resumed her trek, now intending to visit every state capital. Soon, however, she had a new MO: thereafter traveling on horseback, she dressed as a cowgirl, even wearing a sombrero, gauntlets, and spurs. And as a reporter for the *Hartford (KY) Herald* observed on February 14, 1917, "a revolver dangles conspicuously from her trim waist." On February 9, 1917, Skrehot was in Kentucky making her nineteenth visit to a state governor. But there, alas, her newspaper trail comes to an end.

Like Phyllis Skrehot, an ailing twenty-three-year-old Nellie Walker of Portland, Maine, was advised by her doctor to "get into the open" for the sake of her health. Setting out on a trek to the West Coast in April of 1920, she soon found that a worrisome cough and a "heaviness" in her chest were gone. She also found, again like Skrehot, that she enjoyed

Phyllis Skrehot
and her faithful friend "Jennie" on a walking tour of the State
Capitals of the United States. Hike begun from Denver, Colo.
in January 1915 to Pan. Pac. Int. Exposition, San Francisco.
2686

Although Phyllis Skrehot didn't note it on her postcard, her trek was
done to surmount an alleged hopeless case of tuberculosis.

trekking so much that she couldn't give it up. Supporting herself by selling postcards and lecturing in movie theaters, she trekked for six more years, eventually claiming to have covered 40,000 miles through Mexico and Canada and all forty-eight states and, by the fall of 1926, reaching Alaska. In Seward on November 8, however, the United Press reported that an intoxicated Walker had "run amuck," boarding the train to Anchorage and, pulling her revolver, threatening to "clean out the coach." Fined $25 and sentenced to thirty days in jail, she soon found that her trekking career was over.

Also trekking alone in pursuit of improved health was Edith Channel, a forty-year-old stenographer in Kansas City. Told by her doctor that she exhibited the "early stages" of tuberculosis and needed to find a better climate and spend more time outdoors, she took off on foot for San Francisco on February 2, 1915. She financed the trek by selling magazine subscriptions along the way and slept each night at railroad section stations. Following her arrival in San Francisco on July 31, Channel was again examined by a specialist, who found no evidence of tuberculosis and declared hers a case of a "complete cure. The exercise and out-of-doors life accomplished the feat," declared the *Kansas City Times* on August 6, 1915. Maybe so, yet clearly all was not well. On December 14, using the revolver she had carried for protection throughout the 1,811 miles of her trek, Channel sent a bullet through her heart.

The Boy Walker

On August 1, 1908, two young residents of Worcester, Massachusetts, Charles E. Byram and Harry Garrepy, started out from Boston on a walking excursion to California and back. Two uncles in New Haven, Connecticut, had posted $1,000, which would be theirs if they were back within eighteen months and set a record time walking between Boston and San Francisco. When Byram soon pulled out, Garrepy found a new partner, Thomas W. Ray, in New Haven. The trekkers cited improved health as their main goal. Ray, a British subject, claimed to be suffering from the effects of a bullet wound sustained when he fought in the Boer War. Garrepy's problem was an incapacitating case of asthma that had brought his weight down to a puny 105 pounds and made it impossible for him to earn his living by manual labor.

The two men took off on August 25, but within several weeks Garrepy's partner was once again gone, leaving him to trek alone. As he advanced along a southern route to California by way of Florida and the Gulf Coast states, he made colorful claims about his life, and his trek also took on a definite show-biz character. The public learned, for instance, that Garrepy was only nineteen years old and an orphan responsible for the care of two younger brothers and a sister. Unable to work at manual labor, he had cultivated two alternative means of securing an income: singing and high-diving, the latter done under the stage name of Davilo. Tapping these skills for the money needed for his and his sibs' support provided one more reason to undertake his long trek.

Newspaper articles and advertisements amply document the fact that Garrepy, a baritone, got many singing engagements in theaters in cities on his route. Occurring less frequently but doubtless having a bigger payout were the high dives done by the Boy Walker either from a bridge into a river or from a sixty-foot-high ladder into a tub. Garrepy offered three varieties of the latter type: the so-called frog dive, the somersault dive, and, most thrilling, the fire dive done at night. An article in the *Sacramento Union* on July 24, 1909, described the fire dive as follows: "Below him will be a large tank filled with water. On top of it, several inches of gasoline will be poured and lighted just as Harry is about to start on his daring plunge. At the same time his clothes will be inflamed as he fires a pistol just before leaping. Down he will come a rushing

HARRY GARREPY
LONG DISTANCE WALKER, SINGER AND HIGH DIVER.
WORCESTER, MASS

On this souvenir photo card, Harry Garrepy indicated the three fields of endeavor in which he had succeeded in surmounting a debilitating case of asthma.

streak of fire and plunge into the roaring furnace of flames spread over the water tank." The stunt clearly was dangerous; indeed, two months earlier in San Bernardino, Gerrapy had been rescued after striking the water on his side and sinking unconscious to the bottom of the tank,

Garrepy reached San Francisco on June 30, 1909, and began his return trek in mid-July. He claimed to have gained nearly forty pounds, to be "entirely cured" of asthma, and to be "ready for a useful career" once home again. In Akron in mid-December, he told a reporter that he expected to be in Boston to claim the $1,000 by year's end. If he met that deadline, however, no newspaper chronicled it or anything else about him until the fall of 1911, when a Connecticut newspaper reported that he still sang and did high dives for a living. Then, in November of 1912, came word that "Professor" Harry Garrepy was taking his show on the road again, leaving from Boston on a 25,000-mile trek accompanied by a horse and wagon, his wife, and their three children. (Turns out his earlier pose of being single and an orphan and having responsibility for his sibs was malarkey. Also, the Boy Walker was ten years older than he had claimed.)

As of September 30, 1913, the Garrepy family had gone no farther than Trenton, where Harry performed his famous fire dive. His aim slightly off, he struck the side of the tank. Not so lucky this time, he was badly injured, contracted pneumonia, and soon was dead.

Two Novel Health Treks

Trekkers purporting to be walking on their doctors' orders to surmount serious health issues could face a problem: they often looked healthy, even hale and hearty, which seemed to call into question their claims about suffering from ill health. Newspaper articles about trekkers passing through town sometimes included comments along these lines. In the face of this widespread skepticism, however, two hearty-looking trekkers—George E. Pinto and Samuel Pogarman—had long-running success in pushing far-out health claims.

Pinto's story, as it can be pieced together from newspaper accounts, ran as follows. Born nearly totally deaf, he nonetheless learned to read lips and speak normally and graduated from Gallaudet, the well-known college for deaf students in Washington, D.C. He then took a teaching position in the Perkins Institution, a school for the blind and deaf in Boston. Soon, however, his own vision began to fail, the result, he alleged, of an "electrical operation" done to improve his hearing. Finally, in 1911, when he was twenty-three, his vision was so bad that he had to quit his teaching job. Advised by his physician that "his only hope . . . lay in the open air," in early February Pinto sent his wife and son ahead by train and then took off on foot for his parents' home in Kansas City. By his claim, the trekking treatment worked wondrously well; long before his arrival in mid-November, his eyesight was fully restored.

Already a theosophist, a vegetarian, and a marathon runner, Pinto soon added trekking to his list of enthusiasms and began planning a 30,000-mile world tour on foot. For this trek, begun in February of 1914, he made some adjustments to the rationale he had peddled in 1911. As extracted from newspaper articles, his backstory was now this. He was born not deaf but nearly blind, and that "electrical operation" noted earlier was done to improve his vision. The operation succeeded but also "destroyed his hearing." His doctor made the usual prescription of pursuing an "outdoor life." By 1917, Pinto's narrative had acquired new twists: he lost his hearing in 1913, he now claimed in the *Kansas City Times* of July 28, 1917, while playing the piano! Although "a shock of lightning on the Kansas prairie restored it," it was gone again half an hour later when he "fell off a small bridge in the dark." (Had the vision problem also come back?)

Although George Pinto and Samuel Pogarman looked healthy, both succeeded in parlaying claims of bad health into long-running trekking careers.

The inconsistencies and oddities in Pinto's accounts seem never to have been noticed by reporters, who also left unexamined his claim to rely on lipreading. As for his world tour, as late as 1920 Pinto still had not left the United States.

Samuel Pogarman, a Canadian, came on the American scene in February of 1922 when, at the age of twenty-two, he proclaimed his intent to walk from Seattle to New York "just for the fun of it." Like Pinto, he would finance his trek by selling postcards. Four years later, still trekking, he announced that he had covered 15,000 miles through forty-four states and twelve Canadian provinces and expected soon to extend his trek to Europe. He also began to claim that he had enlisted in the British army in 1914 at the outbreak of World War I, was gassed during combat, and was walking for recuperation at the direction of his doctor. By 1928, that story had been filled out in greater detail but also modified in one important respect: sent to a sanitarium at war's end, he claimed, he finally revolted at the prospect of an indefinite stay there and decided on his own—not by a doctor's orders—to go walking to improve his health. As late as 1933, he was still at it but had not yet extended his trek to Europe.

Was Pogarman's story of a near death by gassing and a full recovery by trekking true? Weighing against it was his delayed disclosure of that story. A further problem was that, when he supposedly enlisted in 1914, he would have been only fourteen years old.

CHAPTER 3

Why Trek? Promotions and Whimsies

I N A BRIEF ARTICLE TITLED "Girls Ready to Ride Zebras" published in its February 27, 1915, issue, the *New York Sun* took good-humored notice of a supposed late development in the campaign for women's suffrage. Complicating the efforts of the National Woman Suffrage Association, the article reported, was "an influx of actresses, stenographers, journalists and other professionals, who want to 'go to California.' They have offered to walk the tight rope, ride zebras, 'hike,' or roll all the way across the continent. . . . One vaudeville actress offered to walk all the way to San Francisco if her manager would precede her in a motor car and distribute suffrage pamphlets and literature."

That bit about the actress is plausible; she could easily have put the trek to good use in promoting her own career as well as the suffrage cause. About the other women referred to, however, the article surely got its facts wrong. Any woman having an itch to walk in support of women's suffrage would doubtless have joined the thousands of other women who marched on Washington, D.C., and state capitals and whose collective actions under the leadership of the National Woman Suffrage Association brought about the adoption of the Nineteenth Amendment in 1920. If there were any "girls ready to ride zebras" or any other solitary trekkers crossing the country on behalf of women's suffrage, evidence of them is elusive today. That's also true for any persons who may have felt an urge to trek alone to promote two other big policy struggles of that time: the prohibition of alcoholic beverages via a constitutional amendment and, a few years later, the repeal of prohibition via another amendment.

Yet some were so passionately devoted to causes of special concern that they trekked to advance those causes. One such cause was the Good Roads Movement—that is, the improvement of America's awful roads to make them fit for automobile travel. To promote that cause, in 1914 two young men from Davenport, Iowa, set out on foot for San Francisco, pulling a four-wheeled wagon that was covered with Good Roads promotional materials; they also intended to speak on behalf of that cause as they advanced. (The expedition probably came to an early end, however, after one of the trekkers was badly injured when the wagon tipped over onto him.)

Another trekker pushing for good roads was a bewhiskered U.S. Army veteran, Colonel (so he claimed) Charles Thatcher, who dressed in the frontier manner and stayed constantly on the move in a covered wagon pulled by three mules and adorned with posters, relics, and animal horns and skeletons. From at least 1914 to 1917, Thatcher in his travels also promoted the development of a transcontinental Washington Highway running from New York to Seattle. In that same decade, another trekker, Ezra Meeker, also pushed for the construction of a transcontinental automobile highway that he named the Pioneer Way and specified would follow a combination of two notable nineteenth-century routes, the National Road and the Oregon Trail. Meeker also used his several treks to champion (successfully) the conservation of the Oregon Trail.

Most of the causes propelling trekkers were matters of belief or practice for which their treks provided opportunities for personal testimony or demonstration. Among those using treks in this manner were, for instance, religious evangelists, exhorters of the evils of smoking tobacco and drinking alcoholic beverages, and advocates of a vegetarian diet, including some on each side of the debate over whether fruits and vegetables should be eaten raw or cooked.

Trekking was put into the service of more than lofty causes, however. Also boosted were businesses and products, fraternal organizations, cities and states, and international expositions and other big-time fairs. In these instances, sponsors usually provided some financial support for the trekker or at least the prospect of payment contingent on the trekker's success. Among the sponsors were business corporations, chambers of commerce, city booster organizations, exposition managements, and newspapers and magazines (recall, for instance, the involvement of the *Police Gazette* in promoting treks).

A sponsor committed to putting money into a trek might require the trekker to wear a distinctive shirt or hat bearing the sponsor's name. The trekker might also be required to travel with a suitably emblazoned cart carrying promotional publications for distribution; in accepting sponsorship by a manufacturer of floor sweepers, for example, one trekker even agreed to have his cart designed to resemble a sweeper. Trekkers, primed with information about their sponsors' services, products, or activities, were sometimes also expected to make public presentations about those sponsors as they advanced.

There were also, of course, trekkers walking in pursuit of their own commercial projects. One young man, for instance, had a great idea: walk across the country taking extensive photographs and notes and then later convert all that material into travelogue programs to be presented on the lecture circuit (unfortunately, however, his plan was dashed when someone stole his camera in Tennessee). Another enterprising young trekker took to the road to sell a song he had written, "Remember the Girl in Your Old Hometown," hoping to make it into the next big hit. And some trekkers even combined trekking goals and conventional door-to-door sales—for instance, a married couple identified only as the Two Wonders, who claimed to be walking for a $10,000 prize while selling something called the Waterless Hot Pad.

Another surprising cohort of long-distance trekkers were the just-married couples who used the trek not merely as a trip to a honeymoon destination but as the honeymoon itself. These jaunts typically were projected to last much longer than the usual honeymoon, of course, and a wager, perhaps put up by friends, was also sometimes involved. Although in most cases the answers can't be known today, honeymoon treks pose some fascinating questions. How and why were these treks concocted? Were they entered upon enthusiastically and with full knowledge by both marriage partners? And what impact did they have on the marriages? In at least one case, it's known that the marriage ended after seven weeks of trekking when the bride sneaked away and returned to her parents' home bearing sad tales of a dreadful honeymoon.

Introducing yet another dollop of whimsy into the trekking phenomenon were the treks executed by losers of election bets. Weston, of course, was the first to make such a trek when, having bet on Stephen Douglas to win the 1860 presidential election, he had to walk from Boston to Washington, D.C., to attend Lincoln's inauguration in 1861. By the early years of the twentieth century, the loser's trek was a well-established event, sometimes with such embellishments as requiring the loser to walk barefoot, carry a humiliating sign, or lead a donkey. These long-distance events were only a portion of the burdens that could confront the loser of an election bet, however; other unhappy fates included, for instance, the loser having to push a peanut with his nose down Main Street or transport the winning bettor through town on a wheelbarrow. As silly as these activities were, they do seem to indicate that the political rupture that was the Civil War had healed and that for some, at least, politics was no longer a life-or-death matter.

To promote a cause, boost a sponsor (or oneself), extend a honeymoon, settle an election bet—here were four more identifiable purposes for which sizable numbers of participants hit the trekking trail. Among those trekkers were the following players.

On the Oregon Trail

Soon after marrying in 1851, Ezra and Eliza Jane Meeker moved from Indiana to Iowa to take up farming there, but one harsh winter in the Hawkeye State was enough for them; in April of 1852, with their infant son and Ezra's brother Oliver, they took off for Oregon Territory in quest of free homestead land and warmer winters. Arriving in Portland six months later, they were among an estimated half a million persons who made that trip by covered wagon along the Oregon Trail between 1841 and 1869.

The new arrivals continued to what eventually became the state of Washington, where Ezra successfully pursued a number of business, agricultural, and political ventures in Puyallup and was soon one of the leading citizens. Although he had had only six months of schooling, he was a founder of the Washington State Historical Society, later serving as its president, and in the opening years of the twentieth century he began to write an account of the local and regional history in which he had played so large a part. Meeker also pondered how to ensure that the Oregon Trail and the westward movement it accommodated would not be forgotten. Eventually he arrived at an imaginative plan for highlighting the trail's historical importance and promoting its preservation and its marking: using an ox-drawn prairie schooner, he would retrace his 1852 route, this time going from west to east.

For this expedition, Meeker ordered the construction of a covered wagon comprised of mostly new but some antique parts. After securing and breaking in two oxen and hiring a driver, he departed from Puyallup in January of 1906. Seventy-six years old, with his western frontier garb and long white hair and whiskers, Meeker attracted as much attention as did his schooner and oxen. The trek got enormous newspaper coverage, and the crowds turning out to hear Meeker's many sales pitches often numbered in the thousands. Calling on local leaders, organizations, and historical societies to support his project, he shrewdly solicited only small donations ("nickels and dimes") for the cause but still got many larger ones. Meeker's expedition yielded at least thirty-four large stone markers erected under his direct supervision or put up soon after his departure.

As Meeker trekked east, he spent some time every day writing a book titled *The Ox Team; or, the Old Oregon Trail, 1852–1906*, which

President Roosevelt on His Way to View the Team

Ezra Meeker issued this bizarrely composed postcard to commemorate his call on President Roosevelt in 1907 while on his first cross-country trek.

he published in Lincoln, Nebraska, in October of 1906. Although soon thereafter he reached the Oregon Trail's upper terminus in Council Bluffs, Iowa, he kept going, selling books and postcards to finance his extended trek. Still not hauling up upon arriving at Indianapolis, his old hometown, Meeker continued to move east until he finally reached New York City. Next came Washington, D.C., and a meeting with President Roosevelt, who promised to sign any bill received from Congress supporting the commemoration of the Oregon Trail. (No such bill passed, however.) On his return trip, at St. Joseph, Missouri, Meeker put the schooner, oxen, driver, and himself on trains to Seattle. In July of 1908, two and a half years after his trek's start, he was home again in Puyallup.

Nearly two years later, in March of 1910, Meeker set out once again on another west-to-east trek by covered wagon to continue promoting the Oregon Trail. By the time that trek ended in August of 1912, about 150 markers were in place. Throughout both of his long journeys, he also pursued another objective—namely, the development of a transcontinental automobile highway that would trace the route of the old National Road most of the way from Washington, D.C., to Independence, Missouri, and continue along the route of the Oregon Trail to the West Coast. He dubbed this proposed highway the Pioneer Way. Moving the project to the center of his attention, Meeker must soon have recognized that another trek by prairie schooner made little sense. What was needed was a promotional trip made by automobile along the proposed route. With a driver, he made that trip in 1916 in a Pathfinder automobile loaned by the company, which modified the vehicle to include the canvas top of a prairie schooner.

Although Meeker never got his Pioneer Way, the first transcontinental automobile road—the Lincoln Highway—did follow much of the Oregon Trail across Nebraska. Moreover, after numbers replaced names on U.S. highways in 1926, U.S. 30 provided a reasonably close approximation of the entire Oregon Trail from Council Bluffs west, as did U.S. 40 of the National Road.

Testing the No-Meat Diet

"Not since Weston's time has a pedestrian attracted so much attention," concluded a reporter, probably accurately. He was referring to Mrs. David Beach, whose walk in 1912 from New York City to Chicago got extensive play in newspapers. Two of those newspapers, the *New York Globe* and the *Chicago Daily News*, were sponsors of her trek. When they arranged for Edward Payson Weston to give her some well-publicized coaching sessions, coverage of the trek got off to a very big start.

Often adorning these newspaper articles were photos of an attractive young woman of an unidentified age. As the *Fort Wayne (IN) Journal Gazette* noted wryly on May 24, 1912, "she refuses to pose for a picture unless asked to do so," which she often was. In accord with standard newspaper practice at that time, none of the news articles ever bothered to disclose her given name. Although the Beaches seem to have been persons of some social consequence in New York, those articles also failed to reveal what either did there, other than to assert that Mrs. Beach was "well known in music circles."

What especially grabbed the attention of reporters and the public was Beach's stated purpose for her trek: to demonstrate the validity of her convictions about the merits of a vegetarian diet. She was then writing a book presenting that case and some vegetarian recipes she had developed over the preceding seven years. "I had thought my readers would think I was writing from theory," she explained in the May 13, 1912, issue of the *Lorain (OH) Times-Herald*, "so I decided to prove the truth of my contentions" by making the trek. Her goal, she added in the next day's issue, was "to educate the people to the right way of taking care of their bodies," and for that purpose she gave many talks and interviews touting her dietary convictions as she moved west. Although claiming to be a "vigorous suffragist," she decided not to carry a "Votes for Women" banner to avoid blurring the trek's focus.

Beach left New York City on the morning of April 10, heading north to Albany and then moving west to Chicago, usually on roads but sometimes on railroad tracks. In a limousine following her were a chauffeur, a maid, a representative of the sponsoring newspapers, and ample supplies of vegetarian victuals. She was often met by reporters, gawkers, and local

A *Chicago Daily News* photographer caught a pert Mrs. Beach trekking on Michigan Avenue on May 28, 1912.

bigwigs coming out to greet her and escort her to their fair cities, where cheering crowds usually awaited her arrival.

Every night, before climbing into her hotel bed, Beach had a hot bath, and her maid gave her a rub-down with soothing unguents. In other respects, however, the trek was arduous. Muddy roads and rainy weather were frequent challenges. She was also proceeding on a very meager intake of calories—only two meals a day, each consisting of some combination of small portions of uncooked fruits, vegetables, grains, and nuts. (She dropped milk, cheese, and eggs from the list to demonstrate that no animal products were needed to sustain her.) Concerned about water quality, she drank only pineapple or orange juice or sucked on a lemon.

When Beach arrived in Chicago on May 28, her husband awaited her. Having covered 1,071 miles in 42.5 walking days for a daily average of 25.2 miles, she found that her weight had gone down by fourteen pounds. Soon the Beaches began their chauffeured return trip by auto to New York, from where Mrs. Beach said she would go to their "country place" for the summer. Her book, *My Walk from New York to Chicago*, published in 1914, proved to be an enjoyable read conveying the passionate missionary purpose that had inspired her to trek on behalf of a raw no-meat diet. The book also divulged two secrets: her age was thirty-three, and her full name was Minta Asha Philips Beach.

On June 17, 1913, only one year after Minta Beach's trek, another woman, Gladys Mason, age twenty-two, departed from New York on a long walk that also had the avowed purpose of promoting the "physical culture life," especially a no-meat diet. Like Beach, Mason lectured as she went and ate only two meals a day. However, unlike Beach, Mason maintained that all food for human consumption must be cooked. Although evidence of her westward progression ends in Chicago in mid-September, she had planned to reach San Francisco by Thanksgiving Day. According to the *Sandusky (OH) Register* of August 20, 1913, she had even told their reporter, "I sure can smell that turkey cooking way out in San Francisco town"—certainly a peculiar statement for a vegetarian to make.

Parsnips vs. Pork Chops

Although Minta Beach and Gladys Mason differed fiercely over whether vegetarian fare should be eaten raw or cooked, they demonstrated that both versions of a meatless diet could sustain a long walk. But for most trekkers, might a diet that included meat be better than a purely vegetarian one? As it happened, an investigation bearing on that question had already been attempted in 1911 by Dr. Dudley A. Sargent, director of the "physical department" and gymnasium at Harvard University.

Dr. Sargent proposed to send two men on a trek from the East Coast to the West Coast, one including meat in his trekking diet and the other adhering to a vegetarian diet. According to newspaper accounts, Harvard University funded this study, which presumably included payment of the participants as well as of their expenses. How the participants were chosen is not known but, again according to those news accounts, many candidates were considered. Ideally, what Dr. Sargent needed were identical adult twins whose physical conditions and characteristics were also close to identical. He settled upon two brothers separated in age by two years but otherwise quite similar in physical features.

The brothers, identified as residents of Winchester, New Hampshire, were Jesse Buffum, age twenty-five, and Warren Buffum, age twenty-three. Both were slightly above five feet six, weighed 120 to 125 pounds, and were in excellent physical condition. They also shared an upright walking style that Dr. Sargent favored for its efficiency and likened to that used, he claimed, by many Native Americans. Newspaper articles often identified the brothers as Harvard undergraduates, but their ages and New Hampshire residence weigh against that designation.

Neither of the brothers was a vegetarian, but Warren was assigned that status for the duration of the trek, while Jesse would continue to eat meat as well as other foods. Neither was permitted to drink alcoholic beverages, and both were required to keep detailed daily records of their food consumption and obtain periodic records of their weights and vital signs. For some unknown reason, they were also required always to sleep outdoors, regardless of the weather. When they were in cities, they could rent a hotel room on the condition that they sleep in their sleeping bags on the hotel roof. In Chicago, for instance, they spent a night on the roof of a nineteen-story hotel.

VEGETABLES PROVE BEST
FOOD ON 3000 MILE WALK

Warren Buffum on the Left, W. A. Reynolds, Physical Director of Y. M. C. A., in Center, and Jesse Buffum on Right

As science, the Buffum brothers' competition was a bust, but many newspapers thought otherwise—for instance, the *Los Angeles Evening Herald* on December 19, 1911.

On July 15, Jesse and Warren departed from Boston, taking turns pushing a large-wheeled cart that carried food, sleeping bags, and other supplies. Five months later, in mid-December, they were in Los Angeles, where they reported to Dr. A. H. Reynolds, physical director of the Los Angeles YMCA, who determined that Warren had gained one and a half pounds more than Jesse, his meat-eating brother. Seemingly of greater significance, an exhausted Jesse had had to complete the final 300 miles by train and acknowledged that his brother had held up much better on the trek. An abundance of newspaper articles proclaiming a triumph for vegetarianism soon followed.

Ignoring Jesse's collapse in the final stretch, Dr. Sargent brought forward a different interpretation, however. "The matter of their diet has proved nothing at all to me," he announced. Both men gained over ten pounds on the trek, he noted, greatly lessening the significance of Warren's slightly larger gain. Moreover, at the start he had judged Warren, who weighed several pounds more than Jesse, to be in slightly better condition than his brother; indeed, that was why he assigned the vegetarian diet to Warren, thinking that he could better sustain any shortcomings it might present. But there truly were no shortcomings, Dr. Sargent now revealed, because Warren was permitted unrestricted access to milk, cheese, and eggs. A former vegetarian, Dr. Sargent clearly was pulling for Jesse, the meat eater. He wrapped up the study by finding walking beneficial for both brothers and declared their contest a draw.

The Buffum brothers' trek was clearly a poorly designed scientific fiasco, some of whose flaws the *New York Times* noted in the heading "Two Brothers Wasting Their Time" on November 17, 1911. Dr. Reynolds suggested that more might be learned if the brothers were to walk back to Boston, this time reversing their dietary assignments. The brothers agreed to do so, and an organization in Los Angeles even proposed to fund the return trek, but it seems never to have happened. For its part, too, surely Harvard University was ready to cut its losses.

A Psychological Experiment

Minta Beach had barely completed her trek to Chicago and returned to her home in New York in 1912 when newspapers began to fill with accounts of another woman, Clara Mitchell, walking from New York to Chicago. Mitchell, a young Chicago woman not yet forty who had been a widow for six years, was well aware of her predecessor's accomplishment. Far from being inspired or impressed by that accomplishment, however, she dismissed it as well as Beach's dietary views. As reported in the *Chicago Examiner* on July 15, 1912, Mitchell was eager to "prove to the world that Mrs. Beach . . . is just an ordinary woman and that determination and not diet will enable any person to make the trip." She also made a point of noting that she was trekking alone, unlike Beach, who had been accompanied by a chauffeur and a maid following in an automobile carrying food.

Putting Beach in her proper place was not the main reason that Mitchell decided to make her trek, however. She claimed to have just completed a book-length manuscript on an aspect of early American history. Now she wanted to turn her attention to another area of interest to her—the untapped powers of the human mind—about which she had developed some conclusions. A long-distance walk offered the perfect opportunity to test those conclusions, she recognized. Beach's trek was of significance, then, both for provoking Mitchell to act and for suggesting a method for doing her research. Her trek, she decided, would be a "psychological experiment."

After spending some time at her sister's residence in New York preparing for the trek, Mitchell departed for home on June 20. Upon reaching Chicago thirty-five days later, on July 25, she declared the long walk a great success in providing the evidence she needed to validate three "theories" (that is, hypotheses). The first of these theories was that no special diet was needed for a long trek (this one was aimed at Beach), because physical endurance depends as much on one's mental state as on diet and muscle. Mitchell's successful practice was to eat whatever was available and struck her fancy whenever she was hungry.

Of even greater significance was Mitchell's confirmation of her second theory—that there is a faculty of intuition that can function as a safeguard and a guide. Departing with only $3.50, using no guidebooks or

3,000 MILE HIKE MERELY EXPERIMENT FOR HER

MRS. CLARA MITCHELL.

The *Tacoma Times* on February 5, 1913, was one of many newspapers intrigued by Clara Mitchell and her unusual claims.

maps, and traveling alone and unarmed, she found that her intuition steered her away from danger and toward generous persons who could provide food, shelter, and small donations of money. A reporter for the *Lincoln (NE) Daily Star* on September 30, 1912, described her practice as follows: "Something tells her that within that nice looking farm house is a hospitable family who would be glad to take her in for the night. She walks right up to the door, asks the privilege of resting a few minutes, then the invitation follows to stay overnight." Using this method of "intuitive impressions," Mitchell claimed, she also never made a wrong turn or got lost. But, she noted, that method worked only if "you make the mind quite blank in order to give the right impression time to get in."

The third theory that Mitchell believed her trek established was that "motor action ceases to be an effort when it becomes a habit." This, she claimed, buttressed a conclusion also reached by the late Professor William James of Harvard University. She gave no details, but presumably the book she planned to write would say more about this theory, its significance, and its confirmation by her trek.

One week after her arrival in Chicago, Mitchell decided to extend her "psychological experiment"; several weeks later, again taking only $3.50, she was on her way to San Francisco. But why? She had no more hypotheses to test, but likely she was hooked by the great attention she got from reporters looking for material for feature stories. She continued to provide good copy, too—for instance, walking much of the way in high-heeled shoes, recounting her success in obtaining free meals and lodging, and often dropping the name of Professor James. Trekking by way of San Diego and Los Angeles, she reached San Francisco on April 10, 1913. By her claim, she had gone from New York to that city using only $7.00 of her own money, staying only two nights in hotels, and getting nearly all her meals gratis. It was an amazing achievement. About 400 persons had helped her, and to each she promised to send a free copy of her book. If that book ever got written, however, it seems never to have been published.

Trekking for Jesus and Clean Living

Nurtured by two periods of religious fervor (the so-called Great Awakenings) in the eighteenth and early nineteenth centuries, itinerant evangelism became a familiar feature of American life. Often plying their trade over large territories, some of the early evangelists traveled thousands of miles by horseback each year. Usually having some affiliation with religious organizations, they sought to foster new congregations and strengthen existing ones as well as win new souls for Jesus. In the early decades of the twentieth century, at least three trekking journeys carried on this tradition but brought some new twists to it.

Coming closest to traditional American evangelistic practice were E. G. Smith and Charles Barron, who left San Francisco in the spring of 1914 headed on foot for New York. Smith was a medical doctor and reformed drunkard, but after being born again he self-identified as a missionary, as did Barron, whose only other identification was as a "converted Jew." Although both were affiliated with a large mission in San Francisco, they received no support from it or any other funding source; instead, they purported to follow Saint Luke's directive to "take nothing for your journey," trusting in the Lord to provide. On that basis, they at least got to Fort Wayne, Indiana, where a reporter ascribed a "glad, care-free atmosphere" to their evangelistic work. There, however, the newspaper trail goes cold, which suggests that, their strong faith notwithstanding, they never made it to New York.

Another striking evangelistic trek began on July 3, 1915, when Elmer E. Harkins took off for San Francisco from his hometown of Alliance, Ohio, pushing a two-wheeled cart filled with travel supplies and religious publications. Harkins, who aspired to become a minister, had a connection of some kind with God's Revivalist, a religious publisher in Cincinnati, and with a Bible school in Alliance. As he proceeded, he handed out tracts and preached on street corners on some evenings and in churches on Sundays. Fortifying Harkins's religious impulses were secular allures that affected some of the features and terms of his trek. As reported in a Fort Wayne newspaper, some of "the boys" in Alliance had posted $1,000 that would be his if he completed the trek by Thanksgiving, and if he completed it without selling anything yet ended up with $100, he'd get another $1,000. Neither religious zeal nor financial enticement carried

TWO GOSPEL PILGRIMS WALK AND PREACH FROM PACIFIC TO ATLANTIC.

The long trek of the "gospel pilgrims" likely was over soon after this photo appeared in the *Fort Wayne Sentinel* on May 12, 1914.

EVANGELIST HIKERS—FROM LEFT TO RIGHT, DR. E. G. SMITH AND CHARLES BARRON.

Harkins through, however; upon reaching Chicago, he got married there in December and soon returned with his bride by train to Alliance.

For twelve years, Fred M. Robbins had been a colporteur carrying his wares by horse and wagon throughout Massachusetts, where he was hailed everywhere as the Bible Man. On June 18, 1920, however, full of missionary zeal and accompanied by his son, he left for the West Coast in his Gospel Extension Wagon, on whose sides he had painted attention-getting phrases and biblical references. He intended to return by way of Florida within eighteen months. As he traveled, he planned to preach, hand out religious literature, and cover his costs by selling postcards and Bibles. How well the trek went is not known. However, on

ALL READY! "BE YE ALSO READY."--*Matt. 24:44.*

Above: In addition to selling Bibles, Fred Robbins peddled this postcard on his cross-country evangelistic mission.

Left: As their postcard indicates, the Linebarger brothers took their "strong man and physical culturist" show from Fort Worth to Frisco in their crusade against tobacco and alcohol.

December 17, 1921—a full year and a half after his departure—a newspaper article reported that he had, in fact, gotten to Florida but that two horses had died on the trip.

Not saved souls but healthier lives was the mission of P. A. Linebarger, a bodybuilder who had developed a repertoire of strong-man demonstrations that he employed in the fight—to which he had dedicated his life—against the curses of booze and tobacco. In 1915, at the age of twenty-nine and following nine years of hortatory performances on vaudeville stages, Linebarger took up a wager to trek, accompanied by his brother T. G., from Fort Worth to San Francisco by way of Portland within four months' time. The brothers aimed the trek especially at teaching audiences of boys about the health costs of liquor and tobacco, but they also made street presentations on physical culture topics. Always skillfully entwined with their health messages were demonstrations of amazing physical prowess—for instance, P. A. could bend an iron bar or pull it against six men with one hand or against two men with his teeth. Although the Linebargers were nearly four months late getting to San Francisco, they did draw some great notices in newspapers and—who can say?—perhaps they even rescued a lad or two from the brink of ruination.

Uncle Sam's Recruiters

In the spring of 1913, Sergeant Louis A. Mohr of the 109th Coast Artillery Company, having only a few months left in his enlistment, applied to purchase an early discharge from the U.S. Army. Far from being dissatisfied with his life as a soldier, he greatly valued the four and a half years he had spent in the army. He also believed that many other young men would benefit from military experience and would join the army if they knew more about the features and positive values of military life. But that was why he wanted out early: he had decided to make a one-year trek across the country to provide that information and promote enlistments, and he was eager to get going. His friend Karl Rittman, a sergeant in the Rhode Island National Guard and a professional artist, agreed to join him in this venture.

Mohr's discharge arrived in late May, and on June 15, buoyed by the cheers of a crowd estimated at 5,000, he and Rittman set out on foot from Newport, Rhode Island, for San Francisco. When they reached Albany, Charles F. Saunders, a lawyer in that city, also signed on for the trek. He was not a veteran but wanted to "see the country" and agreed to be the trek's "secretary," taking photos and every night writing up notes about the day's events.

The three trekkers wore U.S. Army field service uniforms and carried U.S. Army forty-pound backpacks and Colt .45 pistols (but not rifles). At night, they camped out and, when necessary, cooked their own meals. They covered from twenty to thirty miles a day, following the army rule of resting ten minutes for every fifty minutes of hiking. Appearing before large, warmly welcoming audiences in YMCAs, armories, and movie theaters, they detailed the everyday life of soldiers, described the army's latest heavy weaponry, and demonstrated the careful design and contents of their backpacks. To cover their costs, they sold postcards, took donations, and developed an amusing vaudeville act drawn from their trek experiences and illustrated with "rapid-fire cartooning" done by Rittman. Taking a route crossing fifteen states, they reached San Francisco at last on May 25, 1914. Regrettably, the book they planned to write using Saunders's notes and photos has not yet turned up.

Mohr, Rittman, and Saunders pitched the attractive features of a soldier's life during peacetime, but within another three years the United

SERGT. KARL RITTMAN   SERGT. LOUIS A. MOHR
CHAS F. SAUNDERS, LL. B.

From Newport, R. I., to San Francisco, Cal.

Wearing army-issue clothing, these three young men trekked across the country selling this postcard and touting the attractions of a soldier's life.

Movie star Dora Rodrigues was photographed when she came through Washington, D.C., on her 1917 recruitment trek. Library of Congress, Prints & Photographs Division, National Photo Company Collection.

States was at war, and voluntary enlistments alone could not quickly produce the large numbers now needed. Yet even as a military draft came into operation, efforts to increase voluntary enlistments quickened, too. Into this intensified national recruitment effort stepped Dora Rodrigues, who in 1917 set out to walk from New York to San Francisco in a campaign aimed at securing 40,000 enlistments for the armed forces.

No more than five feet tall, the diminutive Rodrigues, who hailed from Cincinnati and whose age was somewhere in her third decade, was a movie star in the studio of Republic Films. When the United States declared war on Germany, she aspired to enlist in the navy but pulled back when the recruiter told her that women were used only as stenographers. But when the recruiter chanced to mention that the greatest need was for those who could persuade people to enlist, she saw at once what she should do. Prevailing upon Republic Films to make a two-reel film, *Uncle Sam at War*, for her to show as she trekked, she next persuaded the studio to pay the expenses of their trekking star, who was soon touted on the trek as Dora, the Republic Films Girl.

Rodrigues left New York City in late April, escorted down Fifth Avenue by 10,000 Boy Scouts. She wore the army's khaki hat and uniform, the latter adorned with a banner inscribed "Dora, New York to Frisco, Recruiting 40,000 Men." She was preceded by a press agent and accompanied by a film crew. In the cities on her route, her standard procedure was to set up in theater lobbies, engage young men in discussion, and show her film. Newspapers soon were full of reports of her great success in getting enlistments, but the coverage dried up after her arrival in Kansas City. Although it's not certain that she got to San Francisco, a few later newspaper articles claim that she did. But did she get 40,000 enlistments? That's unlikely but, if a consensus of news articles is accurate, she did reach a respectable 15,000. Coverage of her trek would have made for good reading in the book she said she was writing, but that is another volume whose existence has not yet come to light.

A Walking Advertisement

As the first decade of the twentieth century neared its close, there was much excitement in Oklahoma City, and much to be excited about. In 1907, Oklahoma became the forty-sixth state, and three years later the state capital was relocated from Guthrie to Oklahoma City. The city's chamber of commerce claimed, probably accurately, that Oklahoma City was the fastest-growing city in the United States; in only three years, its population had nearly doubled, climbing from 32,452 residents in 1907 to 64,205 in 1910. The chamber also regularly highlighted the city's many inspiring advances, such as the opening of two large meatpacking plants, the paving of 127 miles of city streets, and the construction of the city's first skyscraper (twelve stories). For sure, everything was up to date in Oklahoma City.

Sharing enthusiastically in the bustle was George Palmer, who had moved to Oklahoma City in 1906 at the age of thirty-two. Where he had come from is not known, but in 1896 and 1897 and then again in 1901, he had been the trainer for the University of Kansas football team in Lawrence. (He lost that job when the training tasks were assigned permanently to the assistant coach.) What he did in Oklahoma City is also not known, but in several newspaper articles he was identified as a "professional pedestrian," the "champion heel and toe walker of the Southwest," and a competitor "in a number of matches in Kansas City." It was in connection with his apparent prowess as a walker that Palmer in 1909 concocted and then presented to the chamber of commerce a scheme designed to spread the word about Oklahoma City as an up-and-coming place.

What Palmer proposed to do was take a long hike throughout the United States, proclaiming the Oklahoma City story in the cities and towns he visited on the way. The specifics were as follows. Palmer would walk from Oklahoma City to San Francisco, continue from that city to New York, and from there return to Oklahoma City, the entire trek to be done within a ten-month period. At all stops along the way he would whoop up Oklahoma City's many fine features and hand out postcards providing supporting data and images. Starting the trek with no money, he would get funds as he trekked solely by the sale of postcards bearing his image. If he completed the trek within ten months and met the other

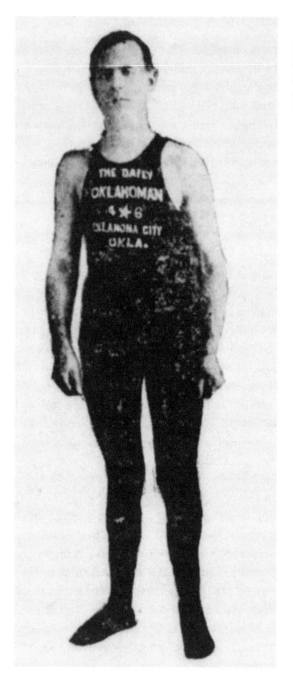

This photo in the *Oxnard (CA) Press-Courier* on February 18, 1910, shows George Palmer wearing the distinctive athletic clothing that he donned for his trek.

conditions, the chamber would pay him $5,000, but if he fell short the chamber would withhold the cash prize and have no other obligations to him. Chamber officials decided to accept his proposal, and soon the city's leading newspaper, the *Daily Oklahoman*, had also signed on as a sponsor.

Palmer set out for San Francisco on December 1, 1909, carrying thirty-five pounds of supplies in a backpack and wearing a shirt bearing the names of the city and newspaper supporting his trek. He was soon adept at making his pitch on behalf of Oklahoma City. A reporter for a California newspaper described him as a "walking advertisement" for that city who "began to boost for it before he had his pack off his back." A New York reporter was also impressed by his boosting talents, noting that he was "out to advertise" Oklahoma City and "has a ready line of talk of the advantages of the place."

Noteworthy, too, was Palmer's great skill in securing support above and beyond the money he got from the sale of postcards. He was a member of the Fraternal Order of Eagles, which had many local lodges throughout the United States, and the trekker planned his route and schedule to take advantage of that fact. Fraternal bonhomie not only took care of a great part of his food and lodging needs but also yielded large sales of his postcards to the lodge brethren.

Palmer reached San Francisco on March 15, 1910, and was soon on his way to New York, getting there in late July. Moving west again, he arrived in Oklahoma City on September 15, sixteen days ahead of his deadline, and was entitled to receive the $5,000. He had covered 8,500 miles on his trek in nine months and fifteen days, which probably was a record of some kind. In the euphoria of that moment, however, he focused instead on issuing a challenge: $50,000 said that he could walk across the country faster than "Rogers, Curtis, or any other" pioneer aviator could cross by airplane. He had no takers.

Apparently abandoning transcontinental trekking for four years, in 1915 Palmer announced that he would try to beat Weston's New York–to–San Francisco time. However, newspaper archives provide no evidence that he ever made this or any other trek thereafter.

Selling a Tuberculosis Cure

As noted in chapter 2, some trekkers believed that long-distance walking was an effective means of addressing serious health problems, including tuberculosis. For three trekkers in 1913, however, the storyline ran in another direction. Certain that they had been cured of the late stages of TB by using a product called Tuberclecide, they were eager to walk from Los Angeles to New York to demonstrate their fully restored health and to urge other sufferers to give this amazing remedy a try. On the way, they also intended to stop off in Washington, D.C., at the White House to solicit President Woodrow Wilson's support for government testing and promotion of Tuberclecide.

Participants in this so-called Transcontinental Endurance Tramp departed from the Los Angeles County Courthouse on April 8, 1913. Accompanying the three former TB patients—two men, Alfred A. Berger and T. J. Price, and one woman, Carrie T. Van Gaasbeek—were Norman A. Clarkson and his sister, Mabel C. Ackerman. At fifty-six, Price was the oldest participant. Three burros carried sleeping bags and supplies for the five trekkers, who camped out most nights. To leave more time to tout the merits of Tuberclecide, the trekkers planned to cover only twenty miles a day and expected to reach New York in December. As they advanced, they handed out postcards and information.

Although he wasn't one of the trekkers, a central figure in this expedition was Charles F. Aycock, who had conceived the trek and enlisted the participants. Owner of the Tuberclecide company and self-declared discoverer of the product's secret formula, he was also a mountebank of the first order and a thoroughgoing cad. Growing up in Arkansas, he worked at various low-level jobs until he was elected treasurer of Boone County. Embezzling county funds, he staged an apparent robbery of his office safe to cover up his theft. The scheme didn't work. Tried, convicted, and sentenced in 1897 to five years in the state penitentiary, he was assigned to assist the prison's physician, which he did for one year.

Contracting tuberculosis symptoms, however, and deemed likely to die soon, Aycock was pardoned in 1899 and given an early release, thanks largely to the efforts of his wife; accompanied by their young child, she had walked throughout the county, getting more than 2,000 signatures on a petition urging her husband's release. Once out of prison, however,

Charles Aycock superimposed his portrait on this postcard depicting the five trekkers who crossed the country promoting his sham medicine.

Aycock ditched wife and child and headed for Indian Territory, which, prior to Oklahoma's statehood, had lax laws governing medical licensing. There he assisted an aged general practitioner and began, by his telling, an investigation and treatment that soon brought an end to his illness and, after fourteen years (so claimed) of dedicated effort, culminated in his miraculous remedy reaching the market in 1910.

In that same year, too, Aycock began a long-running struggle to defend himself against charges that he was a quack and that Tuberclecide was a worthless product compounded mostly of creosote and olive oil. Not until 1928 was he, along with his elixir, finally brought down by actions pursued by the U.S. Post Office. Until then, he had heavy sales deriving from extensive advertising that consisted of big claims, pseudo-scientific jargon, testimonies by grateful users, and angry diatribes by Aycock denouncing his "persecution" by government agencies and the "Medical Trust." Aycock also intended the Transcontinental Endurance

Tramp to be an important part of his promotional campaign. However, even though the walkers completed the tramp, arriving in New York on December 30, their effort didn't get nearly the press coverage Aycock had expected. He added newspaper editors, who otherwise eagerly took his money for ads, to his list of persecutors.

In late November of 1914, Aycock was hit by a legal problem different from the many others he had faced: one of his trekkers, Mabel Ackerman, charged him with breach of promise, claiming that on numerous occasions since 1911 he had promised to marry her and thus, on that basis, she had given him $2,050 and walked across the country at his urging. As recently as early November, Aycock had renewed his pledge to marry her, she also claimed in her suit. Remaining a cad to the end of the chapter, however, in early November Aycock instead married another woman—Carrie Van Gaasbeek, the other woman on the endurance tramp! As one newspaper put it, Ackerman, heartbroken, was seeking a "heart balm" of $25,000. Let us hope she succeeded.

Trekking for Love

Mabel Ackerman, the Tuberclecide walker, was not alone in undertaking a long walk across the country in the pursuit of marriage. Love—or at least the prospect of nuptials—also spurred Charlotte Palmer to make such a walk.

In the spring of 1915, Charlotte Palmer, age forty-five, a resident of Boone, Iowa, and a widow, let it be known that she was engaged to wed Frank J. Foy, age forty-seven, of Vancouver, British Columbia. This appears to have been news to Mr. Foy, who told a reporter that he had never met Mrs. Palmer, although they had exchanged several letters. Whatever the true facts were, Palmer decided to go to Seattle, where Foy was temporarily located, to pursue the marriage. Two sons from her previous marriage—Ed, twenty years old, and Ross, seventeen—would come with her.

Lacking the money to buy train tickets, Palmer decided that she and her sons would make the trip on foot. A long hike, too, might help her younger son's health, which had been impaired by an accident but, according to his doctor, would likely improve with vigorous exercise in the open air. But how would they meet their travel expenses? Palmer came up with a novel plan. Before the family hit the road, she would invite businesses in Omaha to finance the trek on her promise to promote them as the trekkers moved west. To achieve this, the trekkers would follow the recently proclaimed main automobile road, the Lincoln Highway, to San Francisco and then proceed by steamship to Seattle.

Loony though her plan may have seemed, Palmer had startling success in carrying it out. By the time the family (accompanied by their French poodle, Zoe May) departed from Omaha for San Francisco on June 28, she had secured, according to several newspaper accounts, an astounding total of $2,750 from various businesses in that city. Obviously a business genius, she had also arranged to pull in even more money on the trek by selling souvenir cards depicting the travelers. Printed on the reverse of those cards was an advertisement for a chiropractor in Fremont, Nebraska.

Despite its great human-interest value, the Palmer family's trek west got surprisingly little newspaper coverage. From the few available articles come the following items. In addition to a large water canteen and

Met these People on Desert

MRS. CHARLOTTE PALMER and sons,
Ed and Ross, with their little dog, Zoe May,
making an overland trip on foot, over the Lincoln Highway, from Omaha to Frisco. *1915*

Selling this souvenir card was just one of several highly remunerative ways Charlotte Palmer found to finance her and her sons' long trek.

a backpack, each trekker carried a rifle or a revolver. Each (Zoe May included!) also wore an odometer. They walked twenty miles each day, half of that distance in the morning and half in the early evening. And, on behalf of their Omaha sponsors, in the words of the *Algona (IA) Courier* on May 4, 1916, they "painted the names of the corporations on every big rock they passed on their route." (But what else did they do to publicize those firms? Surely meeting their obligation involved much more than defacing the roadside and wilderness!)

Staying at a hotel in Salt Lake City, the trekkers reported having had no troubles or unusual experiences so far on their trek. Several of the other hotel guests then proposed a wager: $250 if they dared to complete their trip without carrying their firearms. Palmer accepted the challenge, of course, but had second thoughts later when the trekkers were menaced by a mountain lion.

After walking 2,500 miles, the Palmer family arrived in San Francisco on October 12. Charlotte Palmer reported that the trip had done wonders for the health of Ross, who had put on 36 pounds—and her weight had moved salubriously in the other direction, falling from 201 pounds to 150 pounds. Because a sizable chunk of their travel money was still not spent, she and the boys were able to enjoy a six-month sojourn in San Francisco before engaging ship passage to Seattle. Arriving at last in that city in April, they found—doubtless to her great relief—that Frank Foy was ready to proceed with the nuptials.

Storm clouds threatened, however, when the judge refused to let the wedding proceed until some local person who knew both parties could testify that they—both well over the age of forty!—were of legal age to wed. But at this darkest hour, as if by a miracle, an old friend of both would-be spouses turned up to make that certification. Wedding bells soon rang out, bringing to a happy ending a charming tale blending romance, shrewd commercial enterprise, and a remarkable trek across two-thirds of the United States.

Honeymoon Hikers

If the honeymoon is intended to get the marriage off to a good start, then the one undertaken by Percy and Beryl Fison, unusual and slightly delayed though it was, seemed to be a real winner. Married in April of 1912 in their city of residence, Colorado Springs, Colorado, this young couple—Percy, twenty-seven years old, and Beryl, eighteen—set out for New York City five months later. Their short stay in that city would be only the second and briefer part of the honeymoon, however; the longer first part was to be the trip there itself, which they intended to make on foot. Because this was the kind of human-interest story the press favored—attractive young couple, apparently very much in love, doing an offbeat thing—the Fisons and their trek received much friendly coverage by local newspapers along the way and in several widely distributed syndicated articles.

Percy Fison had come to Colorado from Jackson, Michigan, by bicycle on a wager in 1910. As a member of the Pikes Peak Athletic Club of Colorado Springs, he had continued to indulge his taste for hiking and bicycle riding. He was identified variously in newspapers as a painter, decorator, or "sign writer." Born in England, Beryl Fison had come to Denver with her parents as an infant, and the farthest she had ever been from that city since then was Colorado Springs, fifty miles distant. When she and Percy met, she was quickly fetched by his smooth talk and athletic exuberance. Soon engaged to be married to him, she eagerly accepted his playful suggestion that they trek to New York on their honeymoon. How this came about was disclosed in a syndicated article appearing in the *Joplin (MO) Morning Tribune* on November 15, 1912: "The long tramp was first suggested by the groom, then a suitor, in a spirit of raillery. 'How would you like to walk to New York?' asked the intended bridegroom, after telling of the joys he had found in long distance walking. 'I will walk anywhere with you,' said the girl blushing. 'You're on,' said Fison." Even if his words had only been teasing ones, he nonetheless accepted, as the article put it, that "he had to make good [about the trek] after he was married."

When friends at the Pikes Peak Athletic Club learned of the Fisons' proposed walk, they passed the hat to raise a prize of $500 to go to them if they completed the walk within ninety days (excluding Sundays).

BRIDE AND GROOM
MR. AND MRS. P. L. FISON
AND 8 MONTHS OLD FOX TERRIER "DUDIE"

Walking from Colorado Springs, Colo., to
New York City in 90 Days

STARTED SEPTEMBER 21, 1912

BRAMBLETT ENG. CO. OMAHA

Percy and Beryl Fison were still love-struck newlyweds when they
prepared this postcard for sale on their honeymoon trek.

Further terms were that the trekkers start out penniless and provide for themselves on the journey only by selling postcards and lecturing about their trek and the delights of Colorado Springs and Pikes Peak. The trek soon became a competition when another young married couple, friends of the Fisons, decided that they, too, would try for the $500 by walking to New York along a different route.

The honeymoon hikers took off on September 21, accompanied by Dudie, their eight-month-old fox terrier. Following train tracks all the way to New York, they averaged twenty-five to thirty miles of walking per day. Never did they lack the funds to pay for food and hotel accommodations; indeed, they pulled in so much cash from the sale of postcards and from lecture fees that they had acquired a surplus of $300 by the time they reached St. Louis! They arrived in New York on January 15, beating their deadline by twenty-two hours and fifteen minutes. Because the other couple attempting the long walk had long since dropped out, the Fisons collected the $500 prize.

To the end, Beryl remained fully enthralled by her trek, telling a reporter that it was the "ideal way to spend a honeymoon." Percy's summation, as noted in the *Philadelphia Inquirer* on January 6, 1913, was less effusive: "While it is a novel way to spend a honeymoon, I can think of better ways now that it is over." He looked forward to spending "that $500 riding back home [by train] in ease and luxury."

Doubtless many residents of Colorado Springs, especially members of the Pikes Peak Athletic Club, were shocked and saddened when, two and a half years later, Beryl was granted a divorce from Percy on grounds of "cruelty." Might Beryl then have reappraised her blissful view of honeymoon treks? Certainly, Percy seems to have changed his view: as the *Golden (CO) Transcript* reported on February 17, 1916, he "must hike back to Colorado to arrange payment of his first wife's alimony before he can continue his second honeymoon." The so-called hiking bridegroom had "started on a second overland trip with a new bride" without making his required payment of $25 to his first bride.

Try, Try Again

Hubert Gottlieb Anton Hassler yearned to find a wife and take a long honeymoon trip on foot or by bicycle. Happily, he found there were young women, usually fresh out of high school, whom he could readily bamboozle into sharing his dream. Three times (at least) within a five-year stretch, he succeeded in snaring a bride. The problem was that each bride's enchantment with the honeymoon trek never lasted very long, and soon she was gone and the marriage was over. Without bothering to get a divorce, Hassler would resume his search for a woman to help him make his dream come true. For that purpose, he usually found it expedient to take on a new name, public persona, or both.

Hassler first came to public notice in late April of 1912, when, at the age of nineteen, he purported to represent the United States in a five-nation bicycle race from Newark to San Francisco and back. Although he spent the next nine months pedaling, he never got west of Denver, but he did make a lengthy trip to Jacksonville, Florida, and back. His shifting accounts of the race's end points, route, sponsor, and prizes indicate that the race, including his claim to have won the first prize of $2,500, was a complete fabrication. However, pedaling through New Brunswick on his return to Newark in late January of 1913, he met Mabel Brodie and instantly knew that here was the real prize.

Mabel was only fifteen years old, but she was already searching for a life beyond the ordinary. Two years earlier she had attempted suicide, explaining to a reporter for the *Newark Evening Star* of February 21, 1913, that "she despaired of ever leading the life of luxury and ease she had often seen in moving pictures." Now came the handsome, smooth-talking Hassler, who proposed marriage and a five-year honeymoon during which they would walk to every state capital. If they succeeded, the Majestic Athletic Association of Jacksonville, he claimed, would pay each of them $5,000. They would support themselves by selling postcards and giving lectures. Not a "life of luxury and ease" but surely a prospect far from humdrum, and so romantic! Astonishingly, Mabel's mother gave her consent, the ceremony took place on February 27, and the happy couple departed on their long honeymoon trek the next day.

Seven weeks later, however, the trek was over, and so was the marriage; in Troy, New York, Mabel sneaked away while Hassler was giving

Mr. and Mrs. Hubert G. A. Hassler on their five year Honeymoon Walking Contest through every State Capitol in the United States on a wager of $10,000 under the Auspices of the Majestic A. A. Started February 28, 1913, New York City without money and selling these Post Cards to cover our expense. Give us what you wish. First Month we walked 326 miles, 13 days Rain, and we wore out two pair of Shoes.

The first of Hubert Hassler's many brides, shown with him on their honeymoon postcard, was gone after seven unhappy weeks of trekking.

a talk and never came back to him. Although crestfallen, Hassler had recovered enough two months later to begin promoting another cross-country scheme: for an alleged $5,000 prize put up by the "Hotel Owners Association of Lake Hopatcong, New Jersey," he would ride his bicycle to San Francisco and back, departing in July and returning by June 1, 1914. Henceforth, he would also be known as Hopatcong Joe. Almost certainly, this new trek was another fabrication; there is no trace of it in newspapers. What is found there instead is evidence that Hassler married again, this time to a woman named Mary, who soon ran off with one of Hassler's friends. When he initiated action against her for bigamy, she did the same against him. Doubtless, both soon dropped all charges.

In 1915, Hopatcong Joe was displaced by Hubert G. A. von Pelt of Vienna. (Hassler's parents were, in fact, Austrians, and he likely was born in Austria.) Now, as von Pelt, Hassler claimed to be on a twenty-five-year bicycle ride around the world that began in 1904 and, when completed in 1929, would yield 25,000 kronen ($6,710). Riding through Pittsburgh, he chanced to meet seventeen-year-old Lauretta Moldausch, whom he married in August. The newlyweds then took off for the remaining years of Hassler's bicycle ride, but by October his bride had tired of the ride and returned to her parents' home. Hassler kept moving, however, and in 1916, now known as James von Pelt McKenna, he announced his involvement in a cross-country ride that also required him to find a bride to win the wager. At least one newspaper reported that he did get married in Chattanooga in the fall of 1916.

A public lecturer rising fast in popularity in 1917 was Professor Hubert Hassler of Vienna, but after the United States entered World War I, the professor became Private Hassler. In April of 1918, however, the army interned the private for the duration of the war, charging him with being a "dangerous alien enemy" (an Austrian) and a bigamist. Reporting this sad event, one newspaper recalled Hassler fondly as a "very bright young man" who "had supreme confidence in his ability." The bigamy charge was on target, but for the rest, the newspaper's assessment surely rang truer than the army's.

Honeymoon Novelties

Most honeymoon treks were attempts at conventional long-distance hikes, but a few had imaginative twists. The following are three specimens of creative honeymoon trekking reconstructed from newspaper reports.

Married on March 22, 1910, William J. Shaw and his bride (her given name was never disclosed in newspaper articles) left the next day from Rochester, New York, for San Francisco on a honeymoon trip projected to continue around the world, cover 43,000 miles, and last three and a half years. For the entire trip, Shaw proposed to pull his wife in a small four-wheeled wagon that he had bought in a toy store! She would walk no more than one hour each day, and he would cover their expenses by lecturing and selling postcards. But why do this? If they held to these conditions and were back by September 12, 1913, Shaw claimed, they would pocket $4,000 put up by a so-called Pathfinder Club.

Although the thin wheels of their cart cut deep into muddy country roads, within three weeks the newlyweds had nonetheless gotten to north central Ohio, averaging thirty miles a day. Finances were their real problem; they arrived in Norwalk, Ohio, for instance, with only eighteen cents. Now claiming that they were contending for a $12,000 purse, soon they also professed to be totally dependent on the public's generosity, forbidden to work, beg, or sell anything. By the time they reached Iowa, they had ditched the cart and Shaw's wife was accompanying him on foot. Reaching the St. Louis area by late August, they then disappeared from newspapers until April 23, 1911, when a final article reported them to be in—Defiance, Ohio, walking eastward! Clearly, the honeymoon was nearing its end.

Desiring to have a unique honeymoon trip, David and Viola Mac-Fadyen designed one certain to be less grueling and more festive than the Shaws had. They proposed to go from New York to San Francisco in a small prairie schooner pulled by two horses; Viola would drive the team, accompanied by a talking parrot and a bull terrier, while David would walk alongside. They would sleep and prepare meals in the schooner and cover their expenses by selling postcards and giving concerts of popular songs. To facilitate that latter purpose, they brought a piano with them.

The MacFadyens were, in fact, accomplished musicians, Viola a pianist and David a singer at Coney Island in the summer and in places

Although on their honeymoon postcard W. J. Shaw looks ready to pull his
wife around the world in a toy wagon, he soon abandoned that notion.

As their postcard reveals, the MacFadyens made a big production out of their honeymoon trek.

along Broadway the rest of the year. A goal of their trip, they announced, was to provide "good entertainment for the country folk" by bringing them "the latest songs." An advance agent, who also assisted them with all other business activities, traveled with them separately.

On April 8, 1911, about 200 friends and colleagues gathered at Coney Island to bid the honeymooners farewell. By that time, two "theatrical magnates" had put up a $2,000 purse and set a December 1 deadline for the completion of their trek, and the trekkers had also signed a lucrative advertising contract with a shoe company. The MacFadyens followed railroad routes and aimed to cover twenty miles a day. When one of the horses died, they switched to two mules. Encountering no other big problems, the happy honeymooners arrived in San Francisco on November 10, well ahead of their deadline.

When George Kufer, a twenty-nine-year-old typographer, set out from Chicago on April 26, 1909, on a 16,000-mile jaunt on foot throughout the United States, he would, by his account, collect $2,000 from the Shamrock Walking Club of Chicago and another $1,500 from a wager if he completed the walk by October 23, 1910. Love soon complicated matters, however. Stopping at the McCloskey farm outside of Woodville, Ohio, on June 1 to request a glass of water, Kufer was invited to have dinner and spend the night; two days later he was engaged to wed the McCloskeys' sixteen-year-old daughter, Gertrude, and within another several days he was a married man. At first thinking that he would have to quit the trek and find a job, he then "remembered" that his contract provided for an additional $500 if he married a woman he met on the trek. The happy couple were soon on their way, squeezing great publicity out of their story; eventually they had the purported lapsed time between their meeting and their wedding down to half an hour, which they boasted was a world record. One year later, they claimed to have covered 13,800 miles, but there is no newspaper record of the trek's completion.

"Two Donkeys"

The presidential election of 1896 was one of the most spirited and significant in American history. The contest generated a very high voter turnout rate of nearly 80 percent and yielded a Republican Party majority that lasted until the election of 1932 brought a new partisan alignment favoring the Democratic Party. The 1896 presidential candidates were winner William McKinley, Republican, and loser William Jennings Bryan, Democrat. Taking place during a time of slow recovery from a major economic depression, the election turned in part on whether to maintain a money system backed by gold only (McKinley's position) or to increase the money supply (and thereby ease the economy's depressed condition) by backing money with silver also (Bryan's position).

Giving close attention to the campaign was Robert P. Woodward or, as he preferred to be known, R. Pitcher Woodward, a thirty-one-year-old socially prominent and well-heeled resident of Brooklyn, New York—son of a judge, graduate of West Point, and an officer of the Woodward Manufacturing Company, maker of woolen goods. Although he later claimed that he had not voted for Bryan, in newspaper articles Woodward was always identified as a Bryan supporter and, as one put it, a "hot advocate of silver." Whatever the truth was about his political affiliation and views, six weeks before the election he was so convinced that Bryan would win that he accepted a risky high-stakes wager with a friend.

Under the friend's proposed wager, the loser would forfeit $5,000 to the winner unless the loser chose to invoke a nonfinancial option, which was to travel with a donkey from New York to San Francisco. Two further conditions of this option specified that the traveler be costumed in an antiquated top hat and a Prince Albert frock coat (the hat could be pitched once the Mississippi River was crossed) and that both man and donkey wear large goggles. The obvious objective was to make the loser look ridiculous. Nonetheless, upon losing the bet, Woodward chose this option, not only to avoid losing $5,000 but also to promote a book of humor he had just published and to get material for another humorous book about a transcontinental trek with a donkey.

Departing on November 27 from the corner of Broadway and Twenty-Third Street in New York, Woodward was allowed one year from election day in which to complete his journey. He was required to start out

TWO DONKEYS
Pythagoras Pod and his Steed
MACCARONI.
PICK THE WINNER.
OTTO J. FRANK,   PHOTOGRAPHER,   NEW YORK.

Having lost his 1896 election bet, R. Pitcher Woodward walked across
the country with a donkey, selling this photo to finance the trek.

with no more than ninety-nine cents but could thereafter earn money by any "honorable" means; he did so sometimes by chopping wood or doing other odd jobs but more often by lecturing, writing articles for newspapers (under the nom de plume of Pythagoras Pod), and selling souvenir photos. For this send-off occasion, he had ordered a large batch of photos depicting "Two Donkeys" and sold these until he had enough cash to settle with the photographer, who was there awaiting payment. Once another $25 had been raised by the sale of more photos, the donkey was delivered, paid for, and named Maccaroni, and the trek could begin. "Amid cheers from the multitude I rode down Broadway," Woodward later wrote, adding that "it was the most embarrassing moment of my life."

Getting little cooperation from Maccaroni, an exasperated Woodward finally replaced him in Poughkeepsie with another donkey, Maccaroni II. The traveling pair soon encountered such a long stretch of severe winter weather that eleven weeks after the trek's start they were still in New York state. During these early days of the trip, Woodward later acknowledged often being cold and hungry and always "very sensitive to criticism and ridicule." Persevering, however, he eventually surmounted his misery and thereafter "travelled and lived and thrived on 'nerve.'" He also found that the farther west he went, the "easier I made money, and the more favorable the weather."

Woodward eventually got his daily average up to twenty-five miles. Usually he walked beside Maccaroni II, accompanied by Donketo, a dog acquired in New York state. In Cedar Rapids, Iowa, he was joined by Tom Glines, whom Woodward designated as his valet; by then, the caravan included four donkeys. On November 2, 1897, this bizarre group, minus two of the donkeys, arrived in San Francisco, beating the deadline by twenty-two hours. In 1902, Woodward recounted his achievement in 423 pages of a book titled *On a Donkey's Hurricane Deck: A Tempestuous Voyage of Four Thousand and Ninety-Six Miles across the American Continent on a Burro, in 340 Days and 2 Hours, Starting without a Dollar and Earning My Way.*

A Freak Election Bet

Charlie Nigg and four of his friends were having one of their frequent palavers at Bunny Hicks's Big Four barbershop in Maquoketa, Iowa. It was the fall of 1912, and a presidential election was coming up fast. This election differed from the usual one in that three major contenders were on the ballot: the sitting president, William Howard Taft, the Republican Party candidate; Woodrow Wilson, the Democratic Party candidate; and a former president, Theodore Roosevelt, the Progressive Party candidate.

The five friends' attention eventually shifted from the election to the continued popularity of so-called freak election bets—that is, bets in which the losers faced outlandish consequences. Very likely this topic was brought up by Nigg, who soon suggested that they concoct their own freak bet; indeed, he had one to propose. Convinced that the split in the Republican Party between Taft and Roosevelt shifted the odds greatly in favor of the Democrat, Nigg posited that Wilson would pull in 450 of the 531 electoral votes. If Wilson fell short of that total, he said, he would walk to the Pacific coast pushing a wheelbarrow. However, if Wilson reached or exceeded that total, the other bettors (all married and having family responsibilities) would hire someone to make that trek; of course, the obvious hire would be Nigg, a bachelor. In sum, win or lose, Nigg would likely soon be trekking.

Nigg's friends took up the wager. Although Wilson won the electoral vote, he fell short of 450 by 15 votes. Nigg began at once to build a light-weight, easy-to-push wheelbarrow that rolled on a pneumatic bicycle tire. On its bright red sides he inscribed "From Maquoketa Iowa to the Pacific or Bust!" Likely he had contemplated making this trek for quite a while, and he was eager to be on his way.

This determination to take a long trek was not surprising; at thirty-six, Nigg had already done a few other out-of-the-way things and showed a reluctance to stick with any job for very long. After graduating from the Maquoketa high school, he became a tinsmith and then a salesman of bottled soft drinks, but when the United States went to war against Spain in 1898, he immediately enlisted and was eventually sent to the Philippine Islands. When his enlistment ended in 1901, he stayed on for four more years as a teacher and translator, both activities made possible by his having learned Tagalog, the principal Philippine language.

As his 1912 postcard shows, Charlie Nigg hardly looks distraught about facing the long trek required of the loser of an election bet.

(Nigg appears to have had the gift of acquiring languages quickly; many newspaper articles attest that he was also fluent in German and Spanish.) He also prepared and published an English-Tagalog dictionary. After returning to the United States, he followed up in 1911 with another publication, a booklet titled "Practical Short-Cuts in Arithmetic."

Nigg's departure on November 19, 1912, was highlighted by the cheers of a huge crowd of well-wishers, a speech by the city's mayor, and a musical escort to the city limits by the town's band. He started with only $4, but in his wheelbarrow he had large supplies of his arithmetic booklet and postcard photos of himself, sales of which brought in a steady income. Also there were a stereopticon and many slides depicting Philippine scenes; Nigg put these items to remunerative use by presenting travelogue lectures in movie theaters along the way. Sleeping out of doors most nights and taking a southern route to avoid bad winter weather, he made good time, arriving in Los Angeles on March 11, 1913.

Soon—much too soon, he doubtless believed—Nigg was entangled again in ordinary life in Maquoketa; two years later, however, he resumed trekking, this time to Portland, Oregon. Although he had intended to go on to San Francisco, find work on a steamer crossing the Pacific Ocean, and continue across Asia and Europe on a long trek ending in New York, he embarked for France, where he found work delivering supplies to the French army during World War I. When the United States entered the war, he enlisted in the U.S. Navy, serving until discharged in 1919. Five years later, he was on the road again, this time departing from New York on a trek having a serious promotional purpose, as proclaimed on his wheelbarrow: "We Want a USA Merchant Marine." Although San Francisco was his target, a blizzard made him haul up in Wyoming. Nigg made his final long-distance walk in 1928, going from Maquoketa to San Antonio to attend the American Legion national convention there.

Nigg's barrow, which ran over 15,000 miles, is today on display at the Jackson County Historical Society in Maquoketa. It bears Charlie's final, fitting message: "From Iowa Where the Tall Corn Grows."

Barefoot to New York

The presidential election of 1924 certainly lacked the excitement and suspense of the elections of 1896 and 1912. The Progressive Party was again on the ballot promoting a vigorous candidate, Senator Robert "Fighting Bob" La Follette of Wisconsin, who did win the electoral votes of his home state. In marked contrast, however, the major parties put up two lackluster candidates—the sitting president, Calvin Coolidge, the Republican Party nominee, and John W. Davis of Clarksburg, West Virginia, the Democratic Party nominee. Coolidge had been vice president during the administration of President Warren Harding and ascended to the presidency when Harding died in 1923. His candidacy seemed to remain undamaged by the subsequent revelations of the corruption of high-ranking figures in the Harding administration. Although Davis had been the solicitor general of the United States, the ambassador to Great Britain, and a member of Congress, he was not widely known and had been nominated as a compromise candidate on the 103rd ballot by an exhausted national party convention. He lost overwhelmingly in both the popular and the electoral votes.

That Davis's electoral prospects were slim would have been obvious to any calm observer, but that was not Robert A. Loar of Morgantown, West Virginia. A lawyer and an ardent Democrat, he had previously lived in Clarksburg and very likely knew Davis both socially and professionally. When Loar's friend Gene Arnett, a Republican, thought the election called for a friendly wager, Loar eagerly agreed. What Arnett proposed was that whoever lost the bet on the 1924 presidential election would have to vote for the winning party's ticket in the 1928 election (and this would be done in the presence of two witnesses to ensure that there was no cheating). If that penalty was too odious for the loser to bear, he would instead walk from Morgantown to New York City in 1925—or, more precisely, allowing for the mountain range between those two cities, he would walk at least 400 of those miles, the remaining miles to be done by any other means. The real kicker was that all miles were to be traversed barefoot. Rather than vote Republican in 1928, Loar chose this option.

Loar was required to complete his walk by October 1, 1925, or, once again, face the penalty of having to vote for the Republican ticket in 1928. Breaking his leg in a car accident soon after the election, he got a

On September 11, 1925, the *Washington Evening Star* published this image of Robert Loar making his barefoot way through the national capital.

later-than-expected start in training for the big walk, but by late August he was ready to go. According to the *Charleston (WV) Daily Mail* of August 23, 1925, "he has taken much of the summer to toughen his feet . . . with the result that his pedal extremities have almost developed macropodia."

Because Mrs. Loar objected stoutly to her husband making himself conspicuous in their hometown, the trek's starting point was relocated from Morgantown to Fairmont. There, in front of the county courthouse, the trek began on the morning of August 25. Loar showed up smoking a big cigar and wearing a shirt, necktie, straw hat, knickers, and leggings but no shoes or socks. Several hundred persons were there to cheer him on. Required to start with no money and subsist thereafter only on earnings and donations, Loar made a big show of emptying his pockets of thirteen pennies, which he threw to the crowd. After he and several others spoke briefly, a hat was passed and, with $20 now in his pocket, the barefoot walker took off.

Loar had carefully prepared his itinerary by making advance arrangements to speak to many Democratic Party gatherings, where he could also expect to collect ample donations. His bare feet caused much surprise and comment everywhere, of course, and in a hotel in Washington, D.C., he was required to wear shoes in the public areas. In the mountains, he sometimes accepted lifts in automobiles, but otherwise he stayed on foot, his pedometer registering a total of 410 miles (an average of 23 miles per walking day) upon his arrival at Philadelphia. There, having exceeded the trek's required 400 miles, on September 15 he completed the trip by train to New York, where he was welcomed lavishly by the Democratic Party grandees of Tammany Hall.

Also on hand to greet Loar was Al Smith, New York's governor and the Democratic Party's presidential nominee in 1928. Loar appears to have made no bets in that year's election, however—a wise decision, because not until Franklin Roosevelt in 1932 did the Democrats again have a winner.

CHAPTER 4

Trekking as a Lifestyle Choice

THE NEWSPAPER ARCHIVES THAT today make it possible to document successful long-distance treks also give indirect evidence of many failed ones. The latter group includes many treks for which the newspaper trail is meager, often beginning and ending with single articles recording the trekkers' departures. Other likely failed treks are those whose newspaper coverage continued for a considerable distance but then abruptly ended short of the intended destinations.

That many (perhaps most?) long-distance treks were not completed is not surprising. Such undertakings were physically daunting and financially challenging, consumed great blocks of time, and required much careful planning of such matters as routes, schedules, accoutrements, and daily routines. During the years of transcontinental trekking's greatest vogue in the early twentieth century, many enthusiasts probably took it up too eagerly without giving full thought to these realities. The many trekkers claiming to be crossing on wagers often did so under terms that would have further weighed against their prospects of success.

Despite long-distance trekking's burdens and costs, however, many participants did complete their journeys, as the three preceding chapters describe. Even more striking in these pages is the evidence of how often trekkers, once back from their excursions, soon took to the road again to make more long-distance jaunts. Their stated reasons varied—for instance, to continue the recovery of good health, to set new records, to seek funds in support of new schemes, to promote favored causes, or to pursue new realms of show-biz. Very likely there were some undisclosed purposes, too, such as getting back into the limelight and continuing to evade the humdrum routines of everyday life.

Perhaps finding in trekking an agreeable alternative to conventional employment, some persons seemed ready to take it up as a career option or lifestyle choice. Among them were those who stayed on the move for many years, claiming to pursue challenging multiyear treks or even a succession of such journeys in pursuit of big prizes (most of which likely were imaginary, however). Another variant of these careerist trekkers were the so-called globetrotters who proposed to reach every portion of the globe in round-the-world treks, obviously long-term propositions. Usually, these pitches were unrealistic or even bogus (a walk around the world was and remains somewhat daunting to arrange and carry out), but a few persons did get out of the country to continue their treks through other parts of the world. Too, some who crossed the United States on foot were globetrotters whose treks had originated in European countries.

Another category of persons adopting trekking as a lifestyle were those taking it up as a means of coping with misfortune. Sometimes this was a deranged choice made by desperate persons suffering acutely from the absence or loss of a loved one; in one such case, newspaper accounts freely speculated that the trekker was insane, and authorities eventually acted to end her wanderings. In several other instances, however, the trekkers' sad stories and expressions of anguish were faked and used to justify treks that lasted several years or even longer. A final group under this heading consisted of persons having genuine physical disabilities who turned to arduous long-distance trekking as a means of securing a livelihood.

In sum, under the heading of trekking as a lifestyle choice at least three broad categories of participants can be distinguished: persons hooked on trekking, would-be globetrotters, and those (both legitimate and false) who claimed to be suffering from some misfortune.

Sergeant Walsh

"Where can I find a reporter?" the weather-beaten stranger asked the elevator boy at the *Boston Globe's* building on the morning of August 12, 1895.

"Upstairs. Come right in and I will carry you up," the elevator boy answered.

"Excuse me, . . . I can't ride," replied the tall stranger, who then proceeded to walk up six flights to the newspaper's editorial chambers. There he informed the city editor that his name was John Walsh and that he had just walked the entire way from San Francisco to the editor's office. He had done so, he explained, in consequence of a bet made with "the boys" gathered in a saloon back home. Boasting then that he could walk as well as Dan O'Leary, a professional pedestrian, Walsh was immediately challenged: $500 would be his if he could get to Boston on foot within a hundred days. Accepting the challenge, he left San Francisco on May 15 and reached Boston with nearly a week to spare.

Walsh was an early user of the wager-provoked-by-a-boast storyline that was soon cited by many other would-be long-distance trekkers. Because his newspaper trail is meager, however, it is not possible to follow his trek or assess his claim to have completed it in ninety-six days. A few days after his arrival in Boston, several newspapers reported that he had begun walking back to San Francisco, but there is no further press coverage of him or his trek. None, that is, until the fall of 1907, when Walsh once again set out on foot from San Francisco to New York. This time he got lavish newspaper coverage.

What had Walsh been doing during the twelve years separating his treks? And what brought him back to trekking? The answer to the first question is very uncertain. Walsh claimed to have been in the U.S. Army on active duty from 1881 until he retired in 1908 with the rank of sergeant, but that claim collides with the fact of his civilian status when he made his trek in 1895. Perhaps, however, he was a soldier during some or even many of those years, if not all of them. The second question is less of a puzzler. Whatever line of work he had been following, he gave it up permanently in 1907 and stayed with transcontinental trekking full-time until 1916; at the age of fifty-one, he clearly had made a late-stage career change. Perhaps he was inspired to return to trekking by

SERGEANT JOHN WALSH,
The man who brought the flag across
the continent.

Although John Walsh's claims of long military service were questionable, newspapers often portrayed him as the gallant old soldier—as in, for instance, the *Boston Post* on August 12, 1908.

the example of the septuagenarian Weston, who in 1907 repeated the Portland-to-Chicago trek that he had made forty years earlier. Finding trekking hugely agreeable, Walsh managed to squeeze a livelihood from it for nine years.

During those years, Walsh steadily pushed his trekking claims, always purporting to have won big cash prizes, typically $5,000, awarded for achieving record-breaking times between San Francisco and either Boston or New York. But, in fact, he likely had no big winnings or genuine records. Close inspection of his very ample newspaper coverage reveals that he did not always complete his much-ballyhooed, high-stakes transcontinental treks; more than once he ended a trek midcourse, reversed direction, and announced a new destination and cover story. The wherewithal he needed to keep going came not from winning wagers but from selling cards bearing his autograph. A member of four national fraternal organizations, Walsh also had exceptional success freeloading on their local chapters, especially those of the Elks.

Although some newspaper editors (and brother Elks) soon spotted Walsh as a fraud, his sheer brazenness enabled him to keep presenting himself not only as Weston's main rival but also as an old soldier of heroic standing. Always carrying an American flag and dressed in an army uniform, he at first claimed to be freshly discharged after twenty-five years of service. Soon, however, he became Sergeant Walsh, a veteran of the Spanish-American War, still on active duty and assigned by the army to demonstrate the hardiness of the American soldier and to test shoes and boots. His 1895 trek, he now claimed, had been done on military assignment. His military record also began to reach ever further into the past, eventually including service under Custer in the 1870s and even service in the Civil War (he was nine years old at that war's end).

Walsh's best stretcher was his last one, accounting for his exit from trekking in 1916: in pursuit of Pancho Villa in Mexico, he claimed, he sustained two bullet wounds and grave injury when his horse fell off a cliff. He was then sixty years old—or, according to his preferred reckoning, sixty-eight years old.

Dakota Bob

One of the earliest and best-known of the careerist trekkers was a conspicuous character known only as Dakota Bob. Born in Fonda, New York, in 1856, he claimed to have dropped out of Cornell University after a year and a half to pursue adventure in the American West. There, by his own account, during the next two decades he was variously a miner, a cowboy, a stagecoach driver, and a cattle ranch guard. He claimed, too, that he worked for three years with Buffalo Bill as a scout for the U.S. Army during the so-called Indian uprisings and took part in the Wounded Knee Massacre of 1890. A newspaper reporter interviewing him more than a decade later wrote that Dakota Bob carried from this period "a dozen wounds from bullets, tomahawks, knives and sabers," an allegation that ranged even beyond his customary inclination to embellish autobiographical details. However, his claim that the sobriquet Dakota Bob had been bestowed on him by Buffalo Bill may indeed have been true.

Dakota Bob's appearance made him one of the most readily identifiable of the earliest trekkers. To the basic outfit of a cowboy he added a large black sombrero covering jet-black hair that reached to his shoulders. Wrapped around his waist was an American flag, and on his chest was a large array of medals and other items, including, according to a reporter who gave them a close look, a rabbit's foot, a fireman's badge, and a Woman's Christian Temperance Union ribbon (a Taft button was also there during the 1908 election year). Always drawing special notice was his necklace, allegedly given to him by an Indian warrior, on which were strung 128 human teeth (but whose mouths they came from varied with different tellings).

Dakota Bob's career as a pedestrian began in 1897 and ran to 1910, during which time he claimed to have made six transcontinental treks as well as two taken "around the world." What those latter two were is not clear, but he may have been walking in other countries from 1904 through 1907, when coverage of him vanished from American newspapers. Inexplicably, too, he omitted from his summary two treks he claimed to have made from East Coast cities to Mexico City and back. In 1910, he announced that he would make a long walk around the periphery of the United States, but instead he brought his thirteen-year career as a long-distance walker to an end. Throughout those years, he alleged, his

Dakota Bob's postcard shows him adorned with his American flag
and buttons and badges but not his necklace of human teeth.

treks had been backed by a succession of $3,000 wagers made between the presidents of the Waverly Athletic Club of Yonkers, New York, and the Golden Gate Athletic Club of San Francisco.

Newspapers mostly gave friendly coverage to Dakota Bob, often finding him to be likable and picturesque. His accounts of his travels and of his trekking practices, such as his preference for walking at night to escape the day's heat, always made for good copy. Perhaps lulled by his fascinating features, most newspapers put aside their usual skepticism and published his claims without raising questions or making any efforts at fact-checking. The *Trenton Evening Times* on September 29, 1898, was even ready to agree that "his walking record is the greatest in the world."

The few newspapers expressing doubts about Dakota Bob's claims were on the right track, however. A search made today in four newspaper archives brings up many articles about him published during his trekking years, but not one of those articles originated in a newspaper west of the Mississippi River; on his many claimed transcontinental treks he seems never to have gotten beyond the eastern third of the United States. A careful recent examination of his two alleged treks to Mexico also shows that he never got south of the border. And can one really take seriously a scenario of two bettors always ready to wager $3,000 on those many alleged long treks with no questions asked, conditions secured, or results verified?

If Dakota Bob's trekking claims were bogus, it still seems too heavy-handed to call him a fraud—a humbug, perhaps, but it would be even more accurate to call him a gifted performer and a versatile one, too. He did his share of the trekker's customary freeloading, but he also earned money along the way by lecturing, doing a mentalist act, and performing a unique paper-cutting act he had perfected. He made a fine performance of trekking, too. The *Hudson (NY) Columbia Republican* of August 10, 1909, summed him up perfectly: "Bob likes to walk in the moonlight, but he manages to keep in the limelight."

From Sailor Jean to Colonial Jack

In 1903, John Albert Krohn was thirty-six years old and lived with his wife and young daughter in Boston, where he was employed by the *Boston Globe* as a printer. He already had more than $2,000 in his bank account and seemed fully in step with American culture's familiar prescriptions for living responsibly and getting ahead. Many folks must have been perplexed, then, when he abruptly quit his job early that year and announced that he would take a long walk throughout the United States.

Krohn's specific plan was to walk to the capitals of all the states, taking three and a half years and covering 22,000 miles to do so. If he succeeded, he claimed, he would win $5,000 put up by M. E. Morton, identified in newspapers as a "wealthy resident of Boston." Morton would also publish the book that Krohn planned to write about his trek, taking a third of the book's earnings in payment. Krohn characterized the trek as a vacation from his regular work, to which he expected to return.

The long duration and great complexity of Krohn's proposed walk imposed a need for careful planning. He decided that his wife, accompanied by their daughter, should precede him by train, sometimes working as his advance agent and always joining him on Sundays. To meet expenses, he planned to sell souvenir items, including picture cards, commemorative tokens, and small aluminum pin trays. These, as well as clothing and food, would be carried in what Krohn called his trolleyette, a wheelbarrow-like conveyance of his own design, whose frame could be taken apart and used to support a tent. Although he had never been a sailor, he planned to dress as one and adopt the name Sailor Jean, believing that both steps would bring him favorable public notice.

Pushing his trolleyette, Sailor Jean departed from Boston on April 1, 1903, and, as numerous newspaper articles attest, for the next thirty-four months he advanced in close accordance with his travel plan and schedule. As of the opening of 1906, he had visited the capitals of forty states, walked more than 20,000 miles, and needed to complete only 1,400 more miles before the arrival of his October 1 deadline. But then, just as Sailor Jean was on the verge of successfully wrapping up this challenging project, he disappeared from further accounts in newspapers. This abrupt and complete ending of his newspaper trail surely indicates that he never completed the trek.

John Krohn's souvenir
cards document his bizarre
metamorphosis from Sailor
Jean to Colonial Jack.

"Colonial Jack" and His Wheelbarrow.

"Colonial Jack" left Portland, Me., June 1, 1908, to walk
around the border of the United States and push a wheelbarrow, a distance of 9,000 miles, to be made in 400 days, (except
Sunday) at an average of 22½ miles per day. Starting from
Portland, Me., he followed the northern border to Seattle, Wash.,
thence down the Pacific coast to Los Angeles, Cal., across the
southern boundary to Jacksonville, Fla., then up the Atlantic
coast to Portland. The walk was made in 357 days, at an average of over 25 miles per day, or 43 days ahead of time, thus
making one of the greatest walking feats ever accomplished.

Although Sailor Jean was gone from the trekking scene, after a two-year absence Krohn was back in 1908 in a new guise. This time he proposed to trek 9,000 miles along the periphery of the United States, starting and ending in Portland, Maine. A wager with an unidentified party stipulated that Krohn would receive $1,000 if he completed the trek within 400 days (Sundays excluded); failing to do that, he would forfeit to the other party 2,000 copies of the book he planned to write about his trek. Once again, Mrs. Krohn would precede him by train, heralding his advance with posters and joining him on Sundays. He would carry necessities, postcards, and other souvenirs in the Sphinx, a pyramid-shaped modification of Sailor Jean's trolleyette. Donning a tricornered hat and knee breeches, this time Krohn would go forth as Colonial Jack.

Like Sailor Jean, Colonial Jack was an excellent long-distance walker whose daily stints exceeded his minimum quota of twenty-two and a half miles. Even so, as he neared the trek's end, according to the *Albert Lea (MN) Times-Enterprise* on August 4, 1909, "he became very nervous, fearing lest something should happen preventing him from completing the journey" (a recall, perhaps, of Sailor Jean's fate?). All went well, however, and he was in Portland on July 21, 1909, forty-three days ahead of the deadline.

Krohn proceeded at once to finish writing his book, *The Walk of Colonial Jack*, published in 1910. In his preface, he confessed that he took his long walk as Colonial Jack "to make money by selling my story." On both of his long treks, sales of postcards and trinkets brought in as much as $35 to $40 a week, according to one newspaper article. Filling the Sphinx with copies of his book, he now took to the road for six more years. Although he never got farther afield than some midwestern states, he always proclaimed that he was on a practice run for a trek challenging Weston that he would do "next year." Meanwhile, preceded by his wife, he sold lots of books and gave many illustrated talks in movie theaters about his great 9,000-mile trek.

Lucky 13

Arriving on foot in Brownwood, Texas, on April 8, 1927, John F. Belland informed a local reporter that he was headed for Washington, D.C., where on May 13 he would end a round-the-world trek begun exactly twenty-five years earlier on May 13, 1902. He then planned to settle down with his wife and three children in Denison, Texas. That was a huge whopper about his trek's starting date, however; the true date was May 13, 1914. Belland's next thirteen years were also marked by some questionable claims and convenient revisions of facts, as well as by stellar performances by a gifted showman.

Belland credited his wife with suggesting in 1912 that they take a walking tour of the world, but he soon made that notion his own, going at it with fervor. They then lived in Portland, Michigan, where Belland owned and operated a publishing company. Selling the business, he and his wife moved to Washington, D.C., where Belland spent more than a year planning the trek's itinerary and looking for persons willing to back it with money. He later gave several differing accounts of who the financial participants were (a "wealthy citizen of Washington," miscellaneous friends and business acquaintances, and commercial clubs in four eastern cities). The scheme he finally announced required the Bellands to post $17,500, to be forfeited if they failed to complete the trek or meet every one of its requirements; however, if they completed the trek and met all contractual terms, $110,000 would be theirs.

The Bellands' challenge was to reach the capitals of sixty-nine countries (and soon they claimed that the state capitals of the United States were also included) and return by January 18, 1920—or, expressed another way, to cover about 58,000 miles on land and 27,000 miles on water within five years, eight months, and five days. For this trek, Belland designed a pull-cart that carried their supplies and could be converted into a six-foot bed with an overhead covering. The trekkers would cover their expenses by selling postcards but would also start with thirteen cents, a nod to Belland's obsession with the number 13. He insisted that the thirteen pennies also bear a 1913 mint date, and, once the trek was underway, he declared that it had really begun on May 13, 1913.

Fortifying the trek with Belland's lucky number 13 did not bring success, however. In July of 1915, the couple claimed to have visited the

John Belland and his wife peddled this postcard on their alleged trek to sixty-nine countries.

capitals of Canada, Mexico, and forty-one states and announced that they would next move on to Central and South America. As of September 1916, however, they were still in the United States, and then they vanished entirely from newspaper notice until April of 1921—that is, for over four and a half years and well past their trek's 1920 deadline.

The resumed newspaper coverage revealed a greatly modified trek. Now its purported deadline was January 5, 1925. Belland was no longer accompanied by his wife, and he neither pulled a cart nor sold postcards. He told a reporter that he was "not allowed to work, beg, borrow, steal, solicit, pose, sell, or lecture, but can accept hospitality." Although visiting sixty-nine foreign capitals in pursuit of $110,000 was still his goal, he claimed that only the visits in the Eastern Hemisphere remained to be done. From 1921 until his retirement in 1927, however, his trekking seems never to have taken him beyond the borders of the United States. Nonetheless, as of 1925 he regularly asserted that his trek to the sixty-nine capitals had been successfully concluded (but said nothing about winning a big cash prize).

Belland always made a big hit when he arrived in towns and cities, as many newspaper articles attest; cashing in on that fact, he ignored the supposed strictures against selling and lecturing. Most articles noted what one called his "wonderful flow of language" and another identified as his ability to tap "all the ologies of a college curriculum." Enthralled, one reporter summed him up as "saturated with originality." Among his many lecture topics were the biblical Book of Daniel, the true birthdate of Jesus (February 4), biblical prophecies of war in 1924, why meat should be eaten raw, and the bearing of the numeral 13 on his life. He also sold copies of his treatise on the "mystery of creation."

Belland's trekking routine included depositing thirteen cents in one bank in every town or city that he visited, a practice grounded in publicity seeking as much as in superstition. Although he never expected to recover the money, it did add up to a substantial amount—nearly $5,000, he claimed. About the fate of that even greater original investment of $17,500, he never gave a report.

The Prince of Peripatetics

When George M. Schilling, age twenty-two, departed on April 20, 1896, on a walking excursion from his hometown of Pittsburgh to San Francisco and back, he pinned to his shirt the many medals he had won in athletic contests and took along a large supply of advertising cards listing all his athletic accomplishments. The cards proclaimed him to

George Schilling could honestly claim on this postcard in 1905 to have trekked on five continents on a global walking tour.

GEORGE M. SCHILLING,
FAMOUS AMERICAN ATHLETE.
WHO HAS WALKED ROUND THE WORLD FOR A WAGER,
and has walked 55,000 miles since August, 1897, having left New York in a newspaper suit and penniless, the only man living who has accomplished this extraordinary feat.

be a "Champion Walker" and asserted that in 1895 he had trekked from Pittsburgh to New York in a record time of nine days. The cards also listed Schilling's impressive track and field records attained in local competitions and noted as well his leap of 110 feet from Pittsburgh's Point Bridge into the Monongahela River in 1894. (He soon beat that record when, upon reaching the Mississippi River on his trek, he jumped 140 feet from the bridge at Clinton, Iowa.) Schilling's cards let it be known, too, that these were achievements of a "one-armed athlete"; at the age of nine (!), he had, in fact, lost his left arm at the shoulder to a machine in an ax factory.

Schilling's trek to the West Coast and back was done on a wager in which a local athletic club would pay him $2,500 if he completed the round trip within ten months. Further conditions were that he start with no money, neither beg nor spend money on the trip, and return with $1,000 earned along the way. When King, the Saint Bernard dog with whom Schilling started the trek, gave out after walking twelve miles, Schilling replaced him with King II, a foxhound, who held up to the trek's end. Often both man and dog went without a meal, and Schilling carried a tent on his back to use when a bed for the night was not offered. To earn money, he sold photos and his cards, gave demonstrations and lectures, and, according to one newspaper article, "in large cities, pose[d] as a [dime] museum freak."

Reaching San Francisco on August 24, Schilling and King II started back to Pittsburgh in September and were welcomed there by a cheering crowd on February 18, 1897, two days before the deadline. Falling several hundred dollars short of the required $1,000 in earnings, however, Schilling failed to collect the $2,500 prize. The *Pittsburgh Dispatch* observed—as cited in the *St. Paul Globe* on March 8, 1897—that "his looks betoken lots of hardships" and that he was "positive that he will never attempt such a very foolish performance again." That resolve faded fast, however; one month later, Schilling announced his plan to take on an even more "foolish performance": a walk around the world.

This ambitious project was proposed by the celebrated Brooklyn Bridge jumper and Bowery saloon keeper Steve Brodie, who backed Schilling in a bet with Charles "Parson" Davies, a New York "sporting man." The walk's main features were the same as those of Schilling's earlier walk—start broke, no begging or spending—but he would now collect

Schilling's attempts at two more global treks were freakish ventures, as these postcards reveal, and both fizzled out fast.

$5,000 if he returned within four years, having also earned $5,000. Hailed by the *Trenton Evening Times* as the Prince of Peripatetics, Schilling started west from New York on August 3, 1897, accompanied by King II. Finding in San Francisco that no ship would accommodate a dog, they walked north, finally securing passage on a ship out of Vancouver. On August 5, 1898, man and dog arrived at Sydney, Australia, where King II was quarantined for nearly a year. During that time—and for the next year as well—Schilling walked through Australia, New Zealand, and Tasmania and even performed with a traveling theatrical troupe.

When Schilling resumed his trek, he followed an erratic route (taken by ship, train, and on foot) that brought him to Japan in late June of 1901, only two months before the end of his four-year time limit. Then came a three-year hiatus during which he was not heard from. When contact was reestablished, he was in Western Europe, bearing tales of having walked in Russia and in various countries in Africa and the Middle East. But what about the trek's lapsed deadline? That had been extended to seven years, he now claimed, but, imprisoned for many months in Turkey, he couldn't meet the revised deadline. His goal now was to tour the British Isles before heading back to New York. Meeting and marrying a woman in England, however, he remained in that country for ten more years. During that time, he attempted two more treks of global scope, but neither lasted long.

Like many other trekkers, Schilling embellished his claims, and much remains uncertain about his treks. If he wasn't truly the Prince of Peripatetics, however, this much can be said: unlike some others claiming to be global trekkers, he at least reached four other continents.

The Autograph Collector

In Croatia, the Mikulec family eked out a meager living as poor farmers. Facing the dismal prospect of being stuck on the farm for the rest of his life, son Joseph decided that he would first like to see something of the world. Departing on February 5, 1906, at the age of twenty-eight, he walked to Lisbon, then worked his way on a ship headed to Cape Town

AROUND THE WORLD

JOSEPH MIKULEC STARTED FROM AUSTRIA FEBRUARY 5, 1906. WILL WALK 25,000 MILES FOR 25,000 CROWNS. SO FAR WALKED OVER 12,800 MILES.

ANNA STIOPU, A POET OF ROMANTIC ROUMANIA, STARTED FROM BUKAREST MAY 2, 1905. WALKED OVER 11,300 MILES.

Joe Mikulec and his bride had big plans for trekking together, but soon after the preparation of this postcard, their marriage was over. Photo courtesy of Russell Rein.

and from there proceeded across the South Atlantic to Victoria, Brazil. After walking in Brazil, Uruguay, and Argentina for six months, he departed by ship, eventually ending up in Philadelphia on April 20, 1908.

In the United States, Mikulec let it be known that he was engaged in a high-stakes trek around the world. The amount of money for which he was walking varied in different tellings, as did its source; sometimes he claimed $2,000 had been put up by Croatian friends as a challenge, but more often he spoke of a $5,000 prize posted by a popular Croatian publication, which he also claimed was his employer and had assigned him to the trek. By this account, he was to start penniless, forgo begging, cover expenses by selling postcards, and walk 25,000 miles within five years—that is, be back in Croatia by February 5, 1911. He would also submit weekly reports and, at the conclusion of his trek, use these reports to prepare a book, which his employer would publish.

Claiming to have lost time traipsing through Brazilian jungles, Mikulec announced that he would cut his walk in the United States short, going only as far as the eastern border of Indiana and returning to New York, where he would catch a ship to Australia. Love intervened, however. Dining in a restaurant in Erie, Pennsylvania, he learned that his waitress, Anna Stiopu, a pretty lass of eighteen, had recently arrived from Romania, where she claimed to have been a champion competitive walker. Disclosing that another condition of his trek was that he come back married, he proposed to her. Because in Pennsylvania her young age posed a problem, they walked thirty miles to Westfield, New York, to be married there the next day. After honeymooning at Niagara Falls, the lovebirds left for New York, there to sail to Australia and to continue around the world. They also prepared a postcard to sell on their forthcoming trek.

Alas, that romantic excursion was not to be. Chancing in July to walk twenty miles with the newlyweds, trekker Dakota Bob (see the second account in this chapter) told a reporter that "they fight all the time" and "I understand they have separated for good." That was so. Jettisoning his bride in Rochester, Mikulec continued trekking alone; in early August of 1908, he was in Philadelphia, announcing his intention to walk west and then continue to Australia and Japan. Upon arriving in San Francisco on January 18, 1909, however, he declared that to win the prize (which he now claimed was $10,000) he needed to take an extended walk

JOE F. MIKULEC

Native of Croatia and a citizen of the United States of America, who is touring the world over and is collecting data to write a book. Across the oceans works for his passage on steamers. En-route gives lectures and makes his expenses with these post cards.

Although Mikulec's many postcards frequently show him covered with medals, likely all were self-bestowed.

throughout the United States to all the state capitals he had not already visited. He devoted 1909 and 1910 to doing that and to completing the naturalization process to become an American citizen.

As 1911 opened, Mikulec let his alleged five-year deadline arrive and pass without comment, but he was soon on his way to Australia at last. For the rest of that year and all of 1912, he trekked through many countries in Asia, and in 1913 he continued his journey in Egypt and much of Europe. The outbreak of World War I in 1914 brought him back to the United States, where he stayed on the move, still claiming to be contending for a big cash prize. A celebrated figure by then, he bore on his chest thirty medals acquired on his walks, and on his hands were two huge gold rings, gifts, he said, from Chief Geronimo.

To document his treks, Mikulec always obtained signed attestations from public officials, among whom were many of prominence—for instance, Presidents Roosevelt, Taft, and Wilson as well as many foreign leaders and monarchs. In 1913, he incorporated these documents into an album, onto whose pages all subsequent messages and signatures were also entered directly. He carried this monstrous album—two feet tall, a foot and a half wide, one foot thick, 2,000 pages long, and fifty-eight pounds in weight—on his shoulder until he finally built a dolly to carry it. Later came a second album and possibly even a third one, as Mikulec expanded his quest for the autographs of persons in all fields of endeavor. At the end of his quest in 1925, he claimed to have 60,000 entries in his albums, surely a record of some kind.

At first, Mikulec had sought autographs to document his treks, but by 1920 they were his true objective. Eventually, even treks gave way to quests for autographs made by train or automobile.

The Lady Globetrotter

Like other women engaged in long-distance trekking with their husbands early in the twentieth century, Lizzie Humphries got second billing, always identified in newspaper articles only as Mrs. Harry Humphries. That identification continued even after Harry deserted her and she struggled on alone, otherwise becoming well known as the Lady Globetrotter. The following account of that ill-fated trek, as well as of the few facts known about her earlier years, draws heavily on research presented by Robert Hamilton in his 2021 book *The Lady Globetrotter: The Story of a Woman's Endurance*.

Born in England in 1883 as Elizabeth Ann Yates, in 1908 Lizzie immigrated to Winnipeg, where she was soon making stage appearances under the name of Elsie Kelsey. Probably it was the pursuit of an acting career that next brought her to New York City, where in 1910 she met and married Harry Humphries, a handsome twenty-seven-year-old British actor who claimed also to be a photographer, an engineer, and a champion long-distance runner. The couple then set out on a round-the-world honeymoon to be done entirely on foot. Upon reaching Florida, however, the honeymooners retraced their steps; two months after their start, they were back in New York. Next came talks with representatives of *Polo Monthly* magazine, following which they again began a round-the-world trek. This one was sponsored by the magazine and offered the prospect of their winning a $10,000 prize.

The trekkers' contract with the magazine specified that they would cover a route totaling 48,000 miles, done mostly on foot, within four years and would send in reports on their journey regularly for publication. Although they could take no money with them, they were permitted to earn money on the trek by lecturing and selling postcards. For the trek Harry, who happened also to be an expert embroiderer, prepared shirts bearing the inscription "Walking 48,000 Miles around the World." Fortified by the hearty support of a large crowd of well-wishers, the trekkers took off from New York's City Hall on July 15, 1911, pushing a small express cart hauling their luggage and supplies. Each also carried a holstered pistol and a knapsack indicating that they were the Kelsey Kids.

Walking first to Toronto, the kids then proceeded to Newfoundland, from there sailed to London, and began their trek through the United

After husband Harry vanished, Lizzie Humphries replaced
their postcard and continued her long walk alone.

Kingdom. Before they were even out of England, however, Harry vanished, taking their meager funds with him. Covering for Harry's sudden absence by claiming that he was felled by "nervous prostration," Lizzie fended off her father's insistence that she quit the trek and resolved to keep going. The contract with *Polo Monthly* held firm, which likely indicated that she had always been the real focus of the magazine's interest in this trek.

After completing her tour of the United Kingdom, Lizzie trekked next through the Scandinavian countries and proceeded to Moscow, her financial situation worsening as she went. Lectures presented in the English language had a narrow range of audience appeal, and she also usually lacked the help of an advance agent. To spice up her talks, she decided to make and show cinematographs (that is, movies) of her trek, but she was often stymied by her inability to get the films until she could pay for them. As Hamilton documents, too, she sent increasingly desperate pleas for money to her father. (Receiving help violated her contract, but likely *Polo Monthly* perceived an interest in keeping the trek going.)

In early December of 1912, Lizzie began to walk west and reached Paris in the early spring of 1914. During the intervening time, one advance agent had disappeared with some of her property; a suitor from the past had shown up, asking Lizzie to marry him, promising financial support for her trek, but then disappearing also; and another advance agent—an employee of *Polo Monthly*—had set off for New York to seek funds from the magazine for Lizzie. She intended to keep going, even though only one and a half years were left in which to cover Africa, Asia, Australia, and South America—two-thirds of the trek. The start of World War I in August of 1914 quickly brought an end to her long journey, however.

Returning to America, Lizzie began a 5,000-mile trek to San Francisco to promote donations to the Red Cross to aid war victims. Newspapers reported that she traveled with an advance agent—her husband, Harry Humphries! Was that truly so? In any event, she soon quit her trek and vanished. Harry married again, twice, and in 1919 he went to prison for trying a short-change scheme in a grocery store.

Lost Souls Trekking

As early as the 1870s, newspapers were taking note of occasional solitary long-distance walkers who were not tramps, settlers moving west, wager-walkers, or other participants in the growing pedestrianism craze. Why these outliers, some of whom were women, were walking across the country cannot always be discerned clearly today, but the stated purpose for at least two of them was to reunite with lost loved ones. (In another instance, however, the walker was a wife trudging from North Carolina to New York to escape from a menacing husband.)

One of these searchers for a lost loved one was Sophie Auguston, but it was not clear whom she was seeking. Born in Sweden, Auguston had immigrated with her parents to Illinois, where her father served as a Methodist preacher in Evanston. In July of 1873, at the age of thirty-eight, she left home on foot, following railroad routes west, and by the next June she was in California. Newspapers there took a great interest in her, but a problem for reporters was the fact that Auguston was tight-lipped and usually refused to speak to them. The reporters' consensus was that her trek was made in search of a miscreant husband, but one thought she had intimated she was pursuing a "gay deceiver" to recover her "lost virtue." Still refusing to say clearly for whom she was looking, Auguston declared in San Francisco that she was "satisfied with her visit" and eager to begin her walk back to Evanston.

Dressed in rags, averse to talking, and, according to one newspaper article, "ugly as sin," Auguston was a pathetic figure widely judged to be insane. Always carrying a Methodist hymnal, she would at times burst into song. Most often she slept in the open. People were often ready to offer her food, but she would usually accept only bread and water and always declined trainmen's offers of lifts on freight trains. When efforts to reach her father in Evanston failed, authorities in San Francisco threw up their hands and sent her to the almshouse, bringing her trek to a sudden end.

In 1910, at the age of ninety-six, Frank Schaum departed from New Orleans for San Francisco on a quest having a clearer purpose than Sophie Auguston's: to find two daughters with whom he had lost contact. A veteran of both the Mexican War and the Civil War, he was operating a bakery in Galveston in 1900 when that city was devastated by a

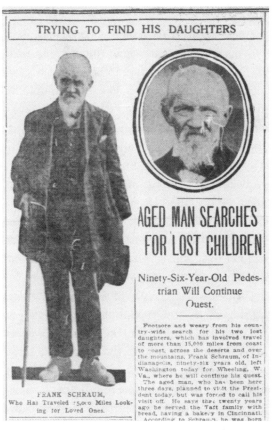

TRYING TO FIND HIS DAUGHTERS

AGED MAN SEARCHES FOR LOST CHILDREN

Ninety-Six-Year-Old Pedestrian Will Continue Quest.

Footsore and weary from his country-wide search for his two lost daughters, which has involved travel of more than 15,000 miles from coast to coast, across the deserts and over the mountains, Frank Schraum, of Indianapolis, ninety-six years old, left Washington today for Wheeling, W. Va., where he will continue his quest.

The aged man, who has been here three days, planned to visit the President today, but was forced to call his visit off. He says that twenty years ago he served the Taft family with bread, having a bakery in Cincinnati. According to Schraum, he was born

FRANK SCHRAUM,
Who Has Traveled 15,000 Miles Looking for Loved Ones.

These illustrations accompanied the sad stories of Frank Schaum and Laura Price (aka Maud Ballard) appearing in the *Washington Times*, May 13, 1910, and the *San Antonio Daily Light*, June 16, 1897.

TRIED TO DROWN HERSELF.

deadly hurricane. After losing his wife, three daughters, and his bakery to the calamity, Schaum moved to New Orleans, where his circumstances continued to deteriorate, prompting him at last to hope that his two remaining daughters, living in San Francisco, could care for him in his last years. Upon completing the grueling walk there, however, he found that his daughters had moved, and his efforts to track them down were unavailing. Undaunted, he began walking east and kept going until he reached Washington, D.C., where he succeeded in obtaining a soldier's pension. When last noted, Schaum was on his way on foot to Sandusky, Ohio, to check into a home for old soldiers there.

Another pitiable wanderer was Maud Ballard, whose goal in trekking seemed to be to end her life—or at least to put on a good show feigning attempts to do so. She and her husband, she claimed, had been circus performers until he died in an accident in 1895. One year later, at age twenty-four, she left New York for Kansas City to look for her sister and brother-in-law. In St. Louis, however, trainmen found her sleeping on the tracks and also stopped her from jumping into the Mississippi River. Walking to Kansas City and then on to St. Joseph, she repeated her tries at suicide by putting herself onto train tracks as well as by attempting to jump into the Missouri River. Whether genuine or not, these suicide performances attracted attention and led to much free short-term board and lodging. During the next two years, she repeated her suicide act several more times, but she always made sure never to do anything that threatened her life until many people were on hand to rescue her.

After walking from St. Joseph to Portland, Oregon, Ballard trekked through California and next ventured east to New Orleans. Returning to California, she found that, even though she had assumed a new name, Laura Price, for the repeat trek there, she was widely recognized as a fraud. She now had to walk less, however, because city officials would often give her a choice: go to jail as a vagrant or accept a fast exit from town by train. By early 1898, her novel practice had come to an end.

Getting to Cedar Rapids

Mr. and Mrs. Harry Krom had a sad story to tell, and it became even sadder in their successive tellings of it. Brazenly pushing their tale of misfortune, they succeeded in sustaining a life of freeloading through many years of trekking.

The Kroms' story began as follows. Until moving to Albany in 1906, they lived in Denver, where Krom claimed to be a cowboy and Mrs. Krom a cowgirl (her first name is unknown, because newspapers never bothered to record it). In 1912, they announced their intention to move to Los Angeles and, in the interest of Mrs. Krom's health, they would get there by walking. Mrs. Krom was, in fact, a frail-looking, diminutive person, allegedly not even reaching five feet in height and described in one newspaper account as a "skeleton of 80 pounds." Once they were on the road, the Kroms provided more details. Mrs. Krom, they revealed, had been suffering from "nervous exhaustion," and her case was so serious that it "had been given up by physicians," who could prescribe only the usual panaceas of fresh air, sunshine, and exercise. Heeding this prescription became urgent by mid-1912, so the story went, when Mrs. Krom's condition worsened following an alleged fire that took the Kroms' house and contents; nothing, they reported, had been insured or was spared.

Taking off in early August, the Kroms announced their intention to reach Los Angeles in five months. Yet, according to a postcard they distributed in 1913, they left Denver on January 1 of that year on a trek to Portland, Maine, in support of Mrs. Krom's health. On the trek they pulled a small railroad express cart carrying a tent, cooking utensils, and postcards and festooned with pennants of the cities visited. Krom announced in Syracuse in late April that the walking treatment had succeeded: Mrs. Krom now weighed one hundred pounds. On June 30, they reached Portland, but three days later they were in Bridgeport, Connecticut, where Krom told a reporter they planned to buy a house and retire.

That was not to be, however, because by early April of 1914 they were on the road again, claiming a need to "get home to the West for the benefit of [Mrs. Krom's] health," but this time their destination was Cedar Rapids, Iowa. Although Portland was identified as their starting point on the first printing of their postcard, on later printings they changed

For reasons not known, Cedar Rapids was the indicated destination on this and several other postcards sold by Mr. and Mrs. Harry Krom on their bogus treks.

that to Salem, Massachusetts, doubtless to tie their alleged house fire to Salem's well-reported Great Fire of 1914. But now their losses to "the fire" were not just house and belongings but also "our baby."

When the Kroms were heard from again three years later, they were in New York City selling postcards outside Saint Paul's Church on Lower Broadway on May 18, 1917, supposedly to raise money needed to walk to Denver. Two weeks earlier, they alleged, they had lost their home in Hartford, Connecticut, its contents, and their two-year-old child to a fire. This sad story was soon countered by the Hartford fire chief's rejoinder that there was no fire or child's death by fire at the time claimed. An undated postcard depicting the Kroms in the later years of middle age suggests that their fraudulent efforts continued at least into the early 1920s. On that card, they professed to be walking from Albany to Cedar Rapids in support of Mrs. Krom's health and—you guessed it—after the loss of their home, belongings, and baby to a fire.

A puzzling postscript to this account of the Kroms' treks was a news dispatch out of Fremont, Ohio, dated July 25, 1929, reporting that Captain Harry Krom, U.S. Army, had made a forced landing of a biplane near there on a flight from Boston to Chicago. But then, on August 6, came a notice of Krom's arrest in Richmond, Indiana, on a charge of obtaining money by short-change artistry and bogus representations as an army captain. His many outrageous claims allegedly included teaching Charles Lindbergh how to fly, accompanying Admiral Byrd to the North Pole, rescuing novelist Zane Grey in the desert, and preparing Amelia Earhart's plane for her trans-Atlantic flight. Asked in court about his trekking years, he said that Mrs. Krom had since died and confessed that there had been no house fires or dying baby. Calling him "the most monumental liar I have ever met," the judge sentenced Krom to six months on a penal farm.

Disabled Trekking

Although the Kroms' claims of being victims of adversity were fictitious, others taking up long-distance trekking had had genuine encounters with misfortune. Among those were persons handicapped by blindness or by loss of limbs. Trekking would clearly have been a huge challenge for them, and the meager newspaper coverage that most got suggests that their trekking efforts were usually short-lived. In at least two instances, however, physically disabled persons did defy the odds and finish long ventures on foot.

One of those successful trekkers was Frank McKeown, self-billed as the Armless Wonder. In 1905, McKeown had, in fact, lost both arms at the elbows to a machine he operated—at the age of thirteen!—in a factory in Passaic, New Jersey. Two years later, on December 24, 1907, the *Philadelphia Inquirer* took note of his booking in a local theater as "an armless carpenter who saws and hammers and chisels with his feet." In his many subsequent performances in theaters and at fairs, McKeown demonstrated a steadily growing set of armless skills, among which, according to his billings, were writing, shaving, using a knife and fork, juggling, shooting billiards, and playing the piano.

Inevitably, McKeown was drawn to long-distance trekking, an activity that could provide a steady stream of new venues and customers for his remarkable offerings. Sponsored by a chewing gum manufacturer, he set out from New York for San Francisco in late October of 1911. Plans soon changed, however, and on January 3, 1912, he again left New York on foot, this time engaged in a $3,000 wager-walk requiring that he make three round trips to Chicago within three years. By mid-1912, he had completed the first round trip, a considerable achievement, but the subsequent four-year gap in newspaper coverage suggests that he didn't do the remaining two. As of 1916, he was mainly engaged in demonstrating his throwing, batting, and fielding skills at baseball games. When the United States entered World War I, McKeown volunteered his services as a cheer-up man in military hospitals, and after the war he became an instructor in physical training for disabled persons.

Also beating the odds weighing against disabled trekkers was Ralph D. Tompkins, who at the age of four had lost his right leg to a freight train while playing in a train yard. In 1911 Tompkins, then eighteen

AT
Foster's Photoplay House
"The Home of Good Pictures"
To-Night
Special Attraction

Frank McKeown
The Armless Wonder

in his great Juggling and Contortion Act. A good 15 minute Act
in ADDITION TO OUR REGULAR PHOTOPLAY PROGRAM. Mr.
McKeown is walking from New York to Francisco. You should
not miss this greatest attraction of the year.

Frank McKeown funded his treks by performing as the Armless Wonder—for instance, at Foster's Photoplay House in Chicago, as this handbill advertises.

RALPH D. TOMPKINS

The only one-legged man who ever attempted to walk
from New York to Chicago. Selling cards
to pay expenses.

Ralph Tompkins relied on the sale of this postcard to meet his trekking expenses
until he found more remunerative ways to cash in on one-legged trekking.

years old and reliant on crutches, accepted a $500 challenge to walk from New York to Chicago and back within four months, a feat that he accomplished. On the day of his departure, July 31, 1911, the *Bradford (PA) Era* described his project as "the latest in freakish pedestrian stunts" and snidely suggested that he would "hop" all the way on his crutches. However, upon his return to New York in December, according to the *New York Times* on December 5, 1911, Tompkins pointed out that "by swinging on my crutches I take bigger steps than the average person and therefore can make quicker time."

In early April of 1912, Tompkins was off again on another round-trip walk, this one between Poughkeepsie, New York, and Jacksonville, Florida. When that trek was done, he left in November on what he said would be a three-year world tour that would start with a swing through all the states. After walking through New York, New England, and some midwestern states in 1913 and 1914, however, Tompkins concluded that, because of the war in Europe, he would continue his stateside trekking but abandon his plan for a world tour. Then, at the end of 1915, he announced that he was tired of long-distance trekking and would give it up altogether.

During those previous five years, Tompkins's circumstances had changed markedly. No longer did he rely on the sale of postcards to meet his expenses. Now he presented travelogue lectures and, having a good bass voice, gave concerts that included singing (and selling) songs of his own composition; at a performance in Bristol, Rhode Island, the *Bristol Phoenix* reported on April 20, 1915, he sold 131 of his song sheets "and could have sold more had his supply not given out." In sum, trekking had brought him public notice, setting him up to make good money, but it had become a burden. Freed from that burden, Tompkins contracted with a vaudeville booking agency and eventually achieved fame as a one-legged jazz dancer. Throughout the 1920s, he also turned his efforts to projects of entertainment and education for children with disabilities.

More Ways to Trek

The allure of long-distance trekking was once so strong that it even attracted persons who had lost the use of both legs either to amputation or to paralysis. These victims of adversity sallied forth in specially constructed conveyances propelled by animals or gasoline engines. Captain Vivian Edwards, a devotee of making long hauls by goat power, was one of these disabled trekkers.

Captain Edwards, a lame fifty-two-year-old breeder and trainer of Angora goats living in Hastings, Nebraska, decided in 1907 that he, his family, and his twelve goats would move to San Diego. (No newspaper article ever explained how he acquired his military title, but several articles made the puzzling claim that he had lost the use of his legs twenty years earlier when he treated a high fever by taking too large a dose of calomel, a purgative.) Sending his wife on ahead by train, Edwards commanded a team of four goats that pulled him in a small four-wheeled wagon. His fourteen-year-old son drove another team of four goats, and the remaining four dutifully followed. Going by way of Oregon, the caravan arrived in San Diego on February 22, 1908, having taken 272 days and covered 4,000 miles.

So swept up by the trekking life was Edwards that a bit more than one month later, on April 1, he and four goats took off again, this time headed for New York. They were accompanied by two men traveling on foot and three burros carrying luggage, camping supplies, photo equipment, and a large quantity of postcards for sale. The stated purpose of the trek was to gather material for the writing of a book. On September 17, 1909, the trekkers and goats arrived in New York, and sometime midway through 1910 they left on their return trip to San Diego. In September, however, the captain contracted pneumonia and died in Uniontown, Pennsylvania. His account of his trek never got written, but lots of his postcards can still be found, certifying to his enthusiasm for trekking despite his disability.

Another partisan of goat power was John Rose, more commonly known as Overland Jack. Born in 1888, Rose, attempting to board a moving train at the age of nine, fell beneath its wheels and eventually had to have both legs amputated. In 1909, shortly after graduating from high school in Delphi, Indiana, the twenty-year-old youth set out to make his way in the world as an itinerant repairman of various everyday items,

Cap. V. Edwards—From San Diego, Cal., to New York. N. Y.

These postcards for Captain Edwards, Overland Jack, and Richard New attest that even persons not able to use two legs could be fetched by the trekking craze.

RICHARD E. NEW
Legless Motor Cycle Rider

such as watches, clocks, and eyeglasses. For this purpose, he drove a small four-wheeled wagon that was designed to let him board and dismount easily, served as his bed at night, and was pulled by as many as five goats.

Eventually operating out of Big Sandy, Texas, where he was affectionately known as the Goat Man, Rose trekked each year through new territory, usually staying on the road from May through October. By the end of his trekking days, he claimed to have covered 30,000 miles and was a well-recognized figure in twenty-six states. As he traveled, he sold postcards at ten cents each or three for a quarter. That practice seemed to have paid off in a very big way; by the time he retired from trekking in 1949, he owned two farms near Big Sandy and had an ample bank account.

Richard E. New had surely followed the most unusual path in legless trekking. While in his early twenties, he specialized in thrilling crowds at county fairs by parachuting from a balloon, but on June 26, 1912, over Dodge City, Kansas, his chute failed to open. Because wires and an awning partially broke his fall of 1,800 feet, he survived, but his back was broken in two places, he lost vision in one eye, and both legs eventually had to be amputated at the knees. Eight years later, in 1920, however, New was back in the public's eye, this time driving a specially modified Harley-Davidson motorcycle. Riding in an attached sidecar, he used hand levers to control his speed and apply the brakes. When not driving, he got around on a small roller chair and at night pitched a tent that used only one pole and five stakes. To cover expenses, he sold postcards. As of early May in 1922, he claimed to have covered 40,339 miles and to be starting on his third trip across the continent.

The hand controls that permitted New's legless excursions could be and still are used in automobiles. But what if the driver's missing limbs were not legs but arms? That problem had also been surmounted by at least two armless drivers trekking throughout the country by automobile prior to World War I.

CHAPTER 5

Exuberant Trekking

IN 1915, THE CIVIL WAR LAY HALF a century in the past, and those fifty years had brought great changes to the United States, which now consisted of forty-eight states reaching from the Atlantic Ocean to the Pacific Ocean. Helping to hold this huge expanse together were recent infrastructural advances—most notably, the construction of telegraph and rail lines that tied all the states west of the Missouri River to the older sections of the country. As of 1914, freight and passengers could move between the two coasts by ship through the just-completed Panama Canal, and the next year brought another big step in national linkage when AT&T initiated long-distance telephone service between New York and San Francisco.

In view of these and other advances, 1915 seemed a good time to celebrate American achievements. In that year, the United States was slated to host a world's fair—the Panama-Pacific International Exposition—which would provide a superb opportunity to tout America's recent accomplishments, especially that most jaw-dropping of them all, the Panama Canal. Held in San Francisco, the exposition also gave the residents of that city the opportunity to showcase their remarkably fast recovery from the devastation caused by the earthquake of 1906. That fast recovery was indicative of a widely prevailing can-do spirit.

San Francisco in 1915 was also the western terminus of the recently proclaimed Lincoln Highway, another great continent-spanning project of that time. Promoted by private citizens who organized in 1913 as the Lincoln Highway Association, the highway was fully realized several decades later as the nation's first paved coast-to-coast automobile highway. In 1915, however, that highway was still mostly an aspiration, barely navigable by automobiles over much of its 3,400 miles. In *The Lincoln Highway: Main Street across America*, historian Drake Hokanson describes one long segment of it as "a mud hole that extended from Illinois to Wyoming." The Lincoln Highway Association nonetheless seized the moment to promote use of the highway for automobile trips to the exposition, and Hokanson estimates that "a handful, perhaps a few hundred" motorists may have made that trip.

Although most citizens would have come to the exposition by train, another handful—but a surprisingly large one—got there on foot or by even more exotic means. Doubtless stimulated by the great fanfare attending the announcements of the exposition and of the Lincoln Highway project, the trekkers turned out in large force in 1915—in fact, the vogue of long-distance trekking very likely reached its apogee in that year. An ongoing search of newspaper accounts published in 1914 and 1915 has already uncovered more than one hundred offbeat cross-country excursions to San Francisco initiated in those years. Most had the stated goal of reaching the exposition, and, all told, they engaged several hundred participants. Many postcards survive, too, that document the fact that the exposition was the destination of many of those transcontinental treks.

Anticipation of the Panama-Pacific International Exposition clearly stimulated the creative impulses of many Americans, as noted in an article published in the *Sacramento Union* on February 8, 1915. Bearing the headline "Freaks Want to Advertise Fair," the article reported that the managers of the exposition had received thousands of proposals for advertising it by means of novel transcontinental excursions. An enterprising resident of Park Ridge, Illinois, for instance, had offered—for a payment of $15,000—to "make a drive across the United States from coast to coast with 150 burros advertising the Panama exposition. On each burro there will be an individual banner advertising some national advertised product and on the stage coach which will be drawn by the burros will be a banner advertising the exposition." Another stunt was offered by a man who proposed to go from San Francisco to New York "locked inside a great iron ball which he would propel from within" and from which he would not emerge until released by the mayor of New York. The newspaper article noted, too, that a widespread rumor—unfortunately false—that the exposition would award a big prize for the most unusual way of getting to the fair had generated hundreds of additional proposals.

Excited by the hoopla attending the coming exposition and, in some instances, bestirred by the mistaken notion that they were competing for a prize, trekkers in 1915 took their proposed transcontinental trips to new heights of zaniness. As in previous years, most of these trekkers were walkers, but not until that year had anyone ever attempted to make the cross-country trip by walking backward, or on stilts, or while pushing a huge hollow steel ball. Also contending for top ranking in novelty was the attempt of two young men to go from New York to San Francisco mostly by canoe (they are known to have gotten at least as far as Jefferson City, Missouri). The many animal-drawn vehicles taking crossers to the exposition included not only the usual wagons hauled by teams of goats, burros, wolves, or dogs but also an elegant chariot pulled daintily by two deer. At least three attempts to reach the exposition were made by pushmobiles, vehicles that advanced by being pushed by partners who alternated every few miles as pusher or driver. Riding a bicycle across the country was old hat by 1915, of course, but among the many cyclists headed to the exposition were two high school boys who scored a first by riding from Washington, D.C., to the exposition and back on a motorized tandem bicycle.

Some trekkers set out for the exposition in inventive groupings. Four young men traveling together covered their costs by giving singing performances under the billing of the Rag Time Harmony Four. Several contingents of Boy Scouts aspired to earn merit badges for skills acquired or demonstrated on the long hike to San Francisco. And eager for a fun-filled trek were some men in Juanita, North Dakota, who proposed to organize as a baseball team and play games against teams encountered as they walked to the exposition. (Newspapers yield no evidence, however, that this scheme was implemented.)

Many trekkers to the exposition purported to be contending for cash prizes, of course; one even claimed that he was guaranteed not only a sum of money but also the hand in marriage of the wagerer's daughter upon completing his trip. Others saw the expedition as a great opportunity to proselytize for favored causes; from one of them, for instance, small-town residents along the way learned why they should adopt military training and daily flag-raising ceremonies in their public schools. Other causes pushed by crossers included improving the efficiency of firefighters by organizing them into two twelve-hour shifts; moving to a back-to-nature diet consisting only of raw cereals, fruits, and vegetables; and—no surprise here—discouraging the use of alcoholic beverages or tobacco products. One antismoking promoter used his cross-country hike as a means (he hoped) of kicking a two-pack-a-day addiction to cigarettes.

Although the fun soon ended when the United States went to war in 1917, the return of conditions of "normalcy" after the war brought a resumption of cross-country trekking. Many of the treks done in the decade of the 1920s displayed the same high level of creativity found in those stimulated by the exposition in 1915. Presented as follows are brief accounts of the treks of some of the ebullient and imaginative Americans who aspired to cross the country in distinctive ways to promote or get to the Panama-Pacific International Exposition in 1915 or who kept trekking's high standards of zany performances alive during the Roaring Twenties.

Checking Out the Lincoln Highway

No one could have been a more enthusiastic recruit for a transcontinental trek than Ed J. Smith, a twenty-year-old resident of New York City. When a friend casually asked, "Ed, how about hiking to the Exposition?" Smith replied, as he reported in an article published in the October 1915 issue of *Better Roads and Streets*, that he "would be there at the start with bells on." His enthusiasm bordered on ecstasy: "For was I not to see America and all her haunts? Was I not to see all those historic places and the wonderful scenic beauty that I had read so much of at school . . . ? Now, I was to walk all over this, and sometimes I really pricked myself to see if I were alive and it were all true." When his fair-weather friend pulled out, the determined young man placed an ad in a New York newspaper seeking a walking partner and claimed to have pulled in nearly a hundred

Smith and Miller Walking Across America.

Ed Smith and C. N. Miller's postcard prompts a question: wouldn't their cart's spindly wheels have sunk annoyingly deep into America's mostly mud roads in 1915? Photo courtesy of Russell Rein.

applicants; he chose C. N. Miller, nineteen years old, to accompany him. After obtaining the well-wishes of the mayor, the duo took off from New York's City Hall on July 15, 1915, pushing a two-wheeled cart carrying their camping gear and proclaiming their intention to see America by walking from New York to California.

Having heard and read much about the recently proclaimed Lincoln Highway, Smith and Miller, in the former's words, "decided to put it to the test"—and, in their judgment, the highway was found wanting. While journeying through Pennsylvania, Smith reported in the article in *Better Roads and Streets*, they were disappointed to find that "the Lincoln Highway signs on the posts were diminishing [in frequency] and we thought if this was happening to the signs, what would happen to the roads?" Becoming increasingly fearful that the Lincoln Highway was more fancy than reality, upon reaching Pittsburgh the two pedestrians abandoned it, proceeded to Washington, Pennsylvania, and there picked up the National Old Trails Road, intending to follow it to Los Angeles. Perhaps that road also posed problems, because upon reaching St. Louis, a newspaper account reported, they continued west on the tracks of the Missouri Pacific Railroad. By October 31, however, they had only reached Sedalia, Missouri. Whether they ever got to the exposition is not known.

The Lincoln Highway Kids

Others had better experiences on the Lincoln Highway than Smith and Miller had—for example, twenty-four-year-old Odowin Doenges of Fort Wayne, Indiana, self-billed as the Lincoln Highway Kid. Doenges claimed to suffer from tuberculosis and to be making the trip to the exposition for the benefit of his health. An ardent member of the Loyal Order of Moose,

FT. WAYNE
TO
CALIFORNIA
AFOOT

Overfield & Doenges
LINCOLN HIGHWAY KIDS
(OVER)

After Bob Overfield teamed up with Odowin Doenges, they prepared this postcard hailing themselves (but not dog Bob?) as the Lincoln Highway Kids. Photo courtesy of Russell Rein.

he got a great send-off by his lodge brothers when he left Fort Wayne on April 4, 1915, accompanied by his dog, Bob. Somewhere along the route he picked up a traveling companion, Bob Overfield, who hoped to surmount heart problems by making the long walk. When sand, blisters, and bad weather made walking across the western desert difficult, the two Lincoln Highway Kids laid up in Eureka, Nevada, for a week but then pushed on, arriving in San Francisco on September 24.

Once done with the exposition, Doenges and Overfield continued by foot to Los Angeles and San Diego; they parted ways when Doenges and dog Bob turned east to follow a southern route back to Fort Wayne by way of New Orleans. After calculating how many miles he would have completed by the time he reached home, Doenges concocted a new moniker: the 10,000 Mile Hiker. As he neared Fort Wayne on April 30, 1916—nearly thirteen months after his departure—the Moose drum and drill team met him at the edge of town and escorted him royally to his house. The trip allegedly did wonders for his health, freeing him from his malady. (Overfield claimed the same good results.) Doenges also gained forty pounds, which may have resulted in part from the free meals he presumably got at the 162 Moose lodges he visited on the trip.

Another self-diagnosed case of tuberculosis treated by hiking to the exposition is worth noting. Samuel H. Cole of York, Pennsylvania, claimed in the *Kennewick (WA) Courier* of March 6, 1914, that his affliction was "in the bones of his feet" and that his method of treatment was to walk the entire trip barefoot. Whether the treatment succeeded is not known, but the news story noted that "Cole's feet have been frostbitten from tramping through the snow."

Frisco Jack, Snookie-Ookums, and Their Pals

The reasons claimed by women for being on the road covered the same spectrum as the men's, including to improve health, to win a wager, to gather material for a book, to see America, and to escape dull daily routines. A combination of all of these, except improvement of health, spurred the decision of Ruth Harsley, Ethel Rockwell, and Maud Bridson—respectively, a cafeteria manager, a hello girl (that is, a tele-

These "nice to look upon" trekkers from Chicago got lots of newspaper coverage—for instance, in the *Centralia (IL) Evening Sentinel* on March 22, 1915.

phone switchboard operator), and a schoolteacher—to walk from Chicago to the exposition. Of all the women on the trail to San Francisco that year, they got the most newspaper coverage, probably for the reason noted by the *Monmouth (IL) Daily Atlas* on March 18, 1915: "The three are nice to look upon. All are under 21." All received frequent marriage proposals on the trip.

The trio left Chicago on March 18, expecting to collect on a $1,000 wager if they got to the exposition by October 1. For security, they carried pistols in shoulder holsters and were accompanied by a collie, Frisco Jack, obtained from the Chicago pound. Carrying camping gear and ready to sleep in the open if necessary, they also hoped to mooch lodging and meals at farmhouses along the way (an objective very substantially achieved) and to raise funds by selling postcards. Although intending to follow the Lincoln Highway, the young women left that road in western Nebraska and reached Denver on April 22. By late June, they were in Salt Lake City, where Rockwell, the hello girl, succumbed to a marriage proposal from a local aviator. Instead of resuming their trek on the Lincoln Highway, the remaining two walkers, accompanied by a new dog named Snookie-Ookums, set out for Yellowstone Park, where newspapers reported that they "chased bears" even though finding them "scary."

The duo next went on to Seattle, arriving there on September 2. Still moving mostly by foot (although throughout the entire trip, they sometimes got lifts from friendly rail crews), Bridson and Harsley got to the exposition on October 1 and presumably collected on their wager. Walking next to San Diego, they turned east there and ended their trip in Kansas City in mid-1916. Although they had much good material for the book they claimed they would write, it seems never to have been published.

By Dog Team to Frisco

Two women are known to have come to the exposition in carts pulled by donkeys, but an animal-drawn expedition undertaken by Estell Mason of Nome, Alaska, certainly topped those trips in excitement and adventure—assuming, that is, that any of her accounts were true. In late 1911, she and her husband, Harry, then performing with Alaskan huskies in an Omaha theater, announced that they were on a worldwide tour pulled by their dogs hitched to a mail sled on which they had replaced the runners with wheels. This trip, allegedly begun in 1908 and already at 10,000 miles, would now continue eastward through Europe, Asia, and Australia and end by May 1, 1915, at the exposition in San Francisco. If they met that deadline (later restated as December 20) and had covered 32,000 miles, they claimed, they would get a $12,500 award allegedly posted by the Dog Merchants of Alaska to secure a test of the "endurance and vitality" of the specific breed of dogs the Masons were driving.

ESTELL MASON and her team of Eskimo dogs left Nome, Alaska, October 27, 1908, for a trip of 32,000 miles around the world, and are scheduled to arrive at the Panama Pacific International Exposition, San Francisco, Cal., not later than May 1st, 1915. She must make all expenses from the sale of these cards and exhibition of her dog team.

Despite the many claims that Estell Mason made on her postcards and elsewhere of trekking in foreign lands, she and her huskies never got out of the United States.

Soon, Estell (unaccountably sans Harry) was on her way with the dogs to New York; however, the troupe stopped frequently to perform and so didn't get there until March of 1913, more than a year later. Although Estell now spoke of a special urgency to get to London fast to advise Sir Ernest Shackleton on the use of dogs in his forthcoming assault on the South Pole, her next reported stop, made in December of 1913, was not London but Philadelphia, and for the next two years newspaper coverage traced her movements west on the final leg of her "worldwide tour." Articles revealed an increasing sensationalism in her presentations, which eventually included terrifying accounts of being lost in Siberia for 132 days and butchering three dogs to feed the other dogs and herself.

In 1915, Mason was last heard from in Shenandoah, Iowa, on October 15, still confident she would get to the exposition to claim the prize. But were there truly a deadline and a prize? And if so, did she collect? The newspaper archives provide no direct evidence. However, she was known to be in California at least as of August 5, 1916, when the *Los Angeles Herald* reported that she had broken her leg and suffered shoulder injuries in Venice when her dogs bolted and threw her from her sled.

ESTELL MASON AND HER MASCOT
MANOFEE

A Good Deed Done

Recognizing a great opportunity to test and hone hiking, camping, and survival skills, a scoutmaster in St. Paul led a group of four Boy Scouts on foot to the exposition in 1915. Two Boy Scouts in Webb City, Missouri, wanting to make a similar trek, on their own worked out an ingenious plan for doing so. Speaking to the city council, Carl Yokum and Cecil Kemper, both sixteen years old, proposed to give their hometown a big

Carl Yokum.   Cecil Kemper.

Carl Yokum and Cecil Kemper's postcard nicely captures their trek's distinctive touches—their Zinc City affiliation and cart loaded with ore samples, their Boy Scout uniforms, and even Cecil's cornet.

boost by walking to the exposition carrying samples of ore from the nearby lead and zinc mines and putting those samples on display at the exposition. To cover the cost of suitable clothing and other initial expenses, they requested an appropriation of $50 from the city council and proposed to meet their other expenses by selling postcards. The city council made the grant, and the publisher of the local newspaper agreed to provide their postcards at no cost.

On March 23, several hundred citizens joined in a parade in the boys' honor, and the next morning they were off, pulling a two-wheeled cart painted red and carrying camping gear, specimens of locally mined lead and zinc, and 5,000 postcards. Moving west through Kansas and Colorado, they headed for Cheyenne, where they picked up the Lincoln Highway for the remainder of their journey.

Upon reaching Sacramento on August 6, the boys were interviewed by a reporter for the *Sacramento Union*, who described them as "brown as Igorrotes" and grateful for their Boy Scout training, which they described as "invaluable in overcoming obstacles on the long tramp." The reporter noted that Yokum had brought his cornet with him and that Kemper "appears to be sick of the trip and is slightly inclined to be surly," not observing, however, that the surliness may have been caused by having to listen to cornet solos. On August 21, the duo had reached the exposition, where, according to one press report, they were "being lavishly entertained by exposition officials," who also put the boys' cart and its contents on display and permitted them to earn money for their return trip by selling postcards. By early 1916, both young men were back in Webb City, hailed as heroes; as the *Joplin News Herald* observed on November 7, 1915, they gave "Webb City as fine an advertising stunt as was ever pulled off."

Pedaling to Frisco

At least two bicyclists pedaled to the exposition in 1915 following the Lincoln Highway the entire way, but they gave markedly different assessments of the quality of their respective rides.

Any bicyclist today would surely balk at having to make a transcontinental ride on the clunker shown on John Bruns's postcard.

Departing on June 7, Howard N. Baker, a twenty-seven-year-old bookbinder living near Boston, reached San Francisco on September 22, claiming to have averaged fifty miles per day of pedaling. An active YMCA member, he found free lodging along the way with many local YMCA chapters. Much of the trip was an ordeal, however. Starting with only $5, he counted on getting more money by selling postcards and doing odd jobs but was often broke and hungry. The highway was often a challenge, too. In Ohio he encountered such massive flooding that he had to walk for fifty-five miles carrying his bicycle on his back, sometimes through waist-deep water, and in Nevada he pushed his bicycle for fifty miles through alkaline dust and sand. Tested by many rough patches of road, his bicycle broke down so many times that Baker declared it only "good for the junk shop" by the trip's end.

John Bruns's bicycle trek to the exposition was a much happier one. Setting out on May 3 from his hometown of Port Jervis, New York, carrying a ninety-pound knapsack on his back, the twenty-six-year-old veteran cyclist declared that he was making the trip "for the education of it." He camped out every night on the way, sold postcards as he went to finance his trip, and claimed to average fifty-six miles per day. Reaching San Francisco on September 3, Bruns proclaimed his bike to be in "good condition" and to have sustained only one tire puncture on the entire trip. The day before, speaking in Sacramento, he also claimed that he was riding on the same tires he had started with and pronounced the Lincoln Highway to be "in such excellent condition" that it was "open even to bicycle riders."

In an earlier dispatch, however, Bruns had noted that rain had caused problems for biking in Ohio, and in a later dispatch sent from Iowa, he reported that, thanks to roads "softened" by rain, "the automobiles leave deep ruts and roughen the roads so badly, we have to walk most of the time." In truth, a bike ride across the United States in 1915 was likely no easier than it had been in the nineteenth century.

A Round Trip by Motorcycle

How would a motorcycle do on a long-distance trip made on roads as bad as America's were in 1915? Bud Baker and Dick O'Brien, recent high school graduates living in Washington, D.C., proposed to find out by riding tandem to and from the exposition on a 1915 twin three-speed Indian motorcycle (it was no more, really, than a bicycle outfitted, in this instance, with a special motor and carrying an extra racing gasoline tank). Starting out on May 3, the young men first dropped by the White House for a photo op and a letter of introduction to carry with them prepared by the president's secretary (citizens once had amazing access to presidents and the White House). Then they were off, reaching San Francisco two months later on July 6. Along the way, they sold postcards of themselves to cover their expenses. A newspaper article reported that they "attracted much attention" at the exposition, where their motorcycle was exhib-

Before starting on their long motorcycle ride, Bud Baker and Dick O'Brien dropped in at the White House. Library of Congress, Prints & Photographs Division, photo by Harris and Ewing.

ited during the week they remained there. Following a more southerly Gulf Coast route on the return trip, they were home again on October 3, precisely five months after the start of their 10,000-mile round trip.

And how satisfying was the trip? Some of the going had been rugged. An account in the *Washington Times* on October 4, 1915, noted that the young motorcyclists "journeyed 600 miles through the desert in Wyoming, Nevada, and Utah [doubtless on the Lincoln Highway] in four days. Leaving Reno, where the thermometer registered 115 degrees above zero, the motorcyclists rode into snowbanks in the Sierra Nevada mountains." The travelers also confessed to having had to use railroad rights-of-way for 400 miles of their travels. Yet they reported having had "practically no mishaps" on the trip, and the motorcycle had not only withstood all challenges, including the cyclists' participation in two races in Chicago and Sacramento, but had also ended "with the same front tire they had started with." As for the young travelers themselves, the *Washington Times* reporter found them "in splendid condition." He wrapped up his story by noting, with a slight hint of envy, that "the dusty and bronzed motorcyclists had many experiences and thrilling episodes to tell their friends."

Chained to His Wheel

Among the true believers in the false report that a sizable cash prize awaited the person traveling to the exposition by the most novel means was twenty-year-old Francis de Lackso of Baltimore. Claiming to have

TRAVELING TO EXPOSITION, CHAINED TO BICYCLE

FRANCIS DE LACKSO.

COAST TO COAST AWHEEL.

This photo of Francis de Lackso, published in the *Washington Evening Star* on March 6, 1915, clearly shows his chained connection to his bicycle.

walked from San Francisco to New York in 1914 (for which there is no newspaper evidence), de Lackso now proposed to make a return trip riding a bicycle to which he was attached by a chain that looped through the bike's frame and ended in handcuffs soldered shut around his wrists. Awake or asleep, he and the bike would be inseparable for the duration of the trip. If he got to the exposition by July 26, so his story went, he'd win a $1,000 prize. Departing from New York City on February 26, he expected to finance the trip by selling postcards, singing, and giving lectures as he went.

His trip was well designed to get ample press coverage, and de Lackso also treated reporters along his route to other gaudy and dubious fare— for instance, he was the son of a French count; he was kidnapped at age seven by a doctor who took him to Brazil, where he worked on a rubber plantation for several years before escaping; then, back in the United States, he met a famed globetrotter who adopted him and introduced him to long-distance walking. His 1914 trek east, he claimed, had taken him into Mexico, where he was impressed into Pancho Villa's army and wounded in battle before escaping.

By May 3, de Lackso was in Omaha, nine days ahead of schedule. However, his plan soon fell apart; not until October, well past his deadline, did he reach San Francisco. Speaking to a reporter there, he said he had been hit by a car in Grand Island, Nebraska, suffering a broken collarbone and internal injuries that put him in the hospital for six weeks, and because hospital personnel were unable to free him from the chain, his bicycle (wheels removed) lay abed with him. Having to abandon his dream of using the (nonexistent) prize to pay two years' college tuition, de Lackso then amended his route to San Francisco; now he would go by way of Spokane to begin recouping financially by picking fruit. Presumably, this meant that he had at last been freed from his intimate connection to his bicycle.

The Stilt King

"On stilts, Harrisburg Man Will Walk to Pacific Coast," read the headline of the March 27, 1914, edition of the *Harrisburg (PA) Telegraph*. The accompanying article reported that F. E. Wilvert, a resident of that city, would depart from it on April 1 and, walking on stilts all the way,

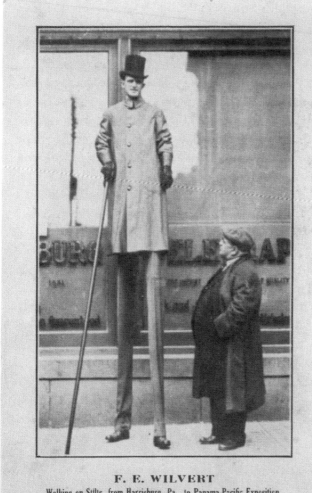

In his postcard image, F. E. Wilvert's top hat adds a few more inches to the great height already reached via his stilts.

F. E. WILVERT
Walking on Stilts, from Harrisburg, Pa., to Panama-Pacific Exposition, San Francisco, Cal.   Height 10 ft. 8 inches.

expected to reach San Francisco by the opening of the exposition in mid-February. Supporting this unusual trek were the newspaper, local chamber of commerce, the Walk-Over shoe company, and the Standard Woolen Company of Harrisburg.

A tailor and ladies' hats trimmer by trade, Wilvert was also an expert stilt walker who had won many competitions. For this trek, he attached Walk-Over shoes to his stilts, wore clothes specially made by the Standard Woolen Company to cover the stilts' length, and carried an eight-foot-long cane, all of which made him look like a stylishly dressed man of ten feet eight. On his back was a banner inscribed "The *Harrisburg Telegraph* extends its greetings to the people of the United States." Wilvert's stated purpose for his trip was to "see the country and get a little experience," and to meet his expenses he sold postcards along the way. From late May on, however, his many public statements revealed his new expectation that he would win a $5,000 prize that he believed was to be awarded for the most original trek to the exposition. Although he got no encouragement in his delusion from exposition officials, he began to send them frequent dispatches about his progress.

Wilvert's wife and children accompanied him, preceding him daily by train. Although one day he covered thirty-nine miles, his daily average was closer to twenty miles. Wind was a special problem, he confessed in Council Bluffs, Iowa, adding that the "trip is anything but pleasant." Nevertheless, he still expected to reach San Francisco by his deadline. All came to an end in early August in Cheyenne, however, when he was arrested and sent back to Pennsylvania on several charges of larceny. According to the *Harrisburg Telegraph* of August 4, 1915, the charges were that he "stole $1.25 from Eliza Reneker and robbed a quarter gas meter at the Metropolitan Hotel annex."

Pushing to the Exposition

On June 20, 1912, two young men, John DeLion of Philadelphia and Simon Schmitt of Toledo, Ohio, began a trip west from Philadelphia by means of a pushmobile that DeLion had built from iron plow wheels,

On these two postcards, John DeLion showed the pushmobile with which he launched his unusual odyssey and its donkmobile replacement.

scrap iron, and sheet metal. This vehicle was powered by one man pushing it while the other man sat within and steered; the two then exchanged
those roles every five miles. Their plan was to go straight to San Francisco,
then take a side trip to Seattle, and eventually return to San Francisco to
attend the exposition. When one of them got sick, however, they put up
in Toledo for the winter and were not back on the road again until July
of 1913. After spending the next winter in Denver, the travelers turned
south in 1914 and ended the year in Optimo, New Mexico, where the
pushmobile broke down.

When the vehicle was ready for use in 1915, however, DeLion's most
recent partner pulled out. Unfazed, he harnessed a burro to push the
vehicle, declared it a donkmobile until a new partner could be found,
and headed south through Santa Fe and Albuquerque to El Paso. At last
reaching Phoenix in early September, DeLion confidently announced
that he would be at the exposition before it closed in December. As
1915 ended, however, the vehicle, once again a donkmobile, was only
in San Diego, and not until September 24, 1916, did DeLion get to San
Francisco, nine months past the exposition's closing and more than four
years after starting from Philadelphia.

During the long trip, DeLion learned ruefully the inherent problem
of travel by pushmobile: it takes at least two persons to make one go,
and while DeLion was steadfast, his partners came and went—all told,
there were ten of them—leaving him frequently reliant on the donkmobile alternative and burdened until he could again find a human
partner. To accommodate successive partners, DeLion also had to make
big changes in his route, and that added many hundreds of miles and
more time to the trip.

In 1915, at least three other pushmobile expeditions set out for the
exposition, each having the advantage of three or four pushers, yet none
appears to have made it past Ohio.

Trekking in Reverse

One cross-country trek made in 1915 reversed the usual direction of movement by departing from the exposition rather than from New York City, but that was fitting, because the man making that trip did so by walking backward. This bizarre undertaking was the product of a friendly dispute between two "club men" of Seattle, both of whom had struck it

Patrick Harmon, Walking Backward, San Francisco to New York

While Patrick Harmon (on the left, presumably) had to sell this postcard and do odd jobs to cover expenses on his backward trek across the country, his watcher had all his expenses paid.

rich in the Klondike Gold Rush. While lounging at the club one day, they overheard another member, Patrick Harmon, boast about his walking prowess. Soon a $20,000 wager had been concocted between the two, centered on whether Harmon could walk backward across the country; if he succeeded, the loser would also have to pay Harmon $5,000.

Accompanied by a watcher, who got $4 per day plus expenses to ensure there was no cheating, the fifty-year-old Harmon left the exposition grounds on August 5, 1915, on his backward jaunt of 3,900 miles that mostly followed the Lincoln Highway. To see the road coming up behind him, he carried a mirror mounted on a pole fastened to his back that projected over his left shoulder. "Panama Exposition to New York Walking Backwards" was inscribed on his knapsack. By selling postcards and doing odd jobs along the way, he earned enough to eat in restaurants and stay in hotels as he traveled. Needing to complete the trip in 260 days to collect his prize, Harmon arrived in New York on May 23, 1916, twenty-one days ahead of the deadline. On days when he walked, he had averaged close to eighteen miles.

Harmon's trek drew much press coverage, including some dollops of derision and even ire. For example, "Not all freaks are in sideshows." Or "What next to keep from working?" Or, best of all, "Because man was created a little lower than the angels is no reason for descending to the level of shellfish." Backward trekking's moment in the sun had arrived, however. In 1923, Jackson H. Corwin, a resident of Philadelphia, also gave it a try, but likely he failed to reach San Francisco. Then came Plennie L. Wingo, who turned to backward trekking after his restaurant failed. Setting out from Fort Worth for New York on April 15, 1931, he continued backward through Germany, Eastern Europe, and Turkey until forced to haul up. After returning to San Francisco, he completed his backward trek to Fort Worth. Wingo's astounding walk is fully recounted by Ben Montgomery in *The Man Who Walked Backward*.

Assisted by special glasses in his backward walk around the world,
Plennie Wingo approached McAlester, Oklahoma, on the Jefferson
Highway in 1931. Photo by Acme Photo.

Gobs on Bikes

The great patriotic fervor that followed America's entry into World War I yielded at least two intriguing transcontinental treks in 1917—movie star Dora Rodrigues's cross-country quest to secure 40,000 Army enlistments (see chapter 3) and an Uncle Sam look-alike's projected hike along a route that would spell UNCLE SAM when laid out on a map. Transcontinental crossings seem pretty much to have vanished during the war years, however. One of the earliest to appear after the war was a cross-country bicycle ride attempted by two navy war veterans, Tony Pizzo, age twenty-three, and Claude Devine, age twenty-one. On May 18, 1919, they took off for New York from Venice, California, after being handcuffed and chained to their bicycles by movie actor Fatty Arbuckle (who also bet $3,500 with a Hollywood friend on the ride's success). Wearing navy garb for the entire trip, they made recruitment talks gratis for the navy and were credited with securing twenty-five enlistments.

Like Francis de Lackso, Pizzo and Devine found that a long-distance ride chained to a bicycle was not an easy go. Believing they were escaped prisoners, a policeman fired his pistol at them. Devine's bike nearly pulled him over the edge at the Grand Canyon. Each man was struck by an automobile and hospitalized on the trip; Devine was injured so severely that his ride came to an end at Kansas City. Continuing alone, Pizzo reached New York on October 31, one day ahead of his deadline.

Following a six-month rest, on April 24, 1920, Pizzo, chained to his bicycle by the mayor of New York, left on another ride, this time to Los Angeles and back. Although he continued to promote navy enlistments, he also aimed to earn money by speaking in theaters and demonstrating such skills as waltzing while chained to a bicycle. Devine, now fully recovered, served as his advance agent. Finishing his ride on November 16, three months early, Pizzo claimed to have won $5,000 in a bet with a friend.

What was left to do? On October 5, 1921, Pizzo pedaled off on a wager to visit every state capital within two years. Again chained to his bicycle, he performed a new dance stunt called the Bicycle Blues. At his last newspaper notice on August 7, 1922, he had reached thirty-one state capitals.

Tony Pizzo and Claude Devine's postcard features them chained to their bicycles while wearing their navy uniforms.

On Rollers across America

Attempting in 1910 to roller-skate from New York to San Francisco (see chapter 1), Max Brody and Abe Levine found that skating was often impossible, and they ended up walking most of the way. In 1921, three pairs of skaters—two young women, two young men, and a husband-and-wife team—resumed the attempt to complete a long trek on skates. All were expert skaters aiming to set a record; no wagers or prizes were involved. Although newspaper archives yield little about the young women's effort, they document amply the fact that the young men completed a round trip on skates between New York and Chicago and that the newlywed couple—Jack and Blanche Carson—skated from New York to the West Coast.

Given that hard-surfaced roads were scarce, especially west of Chicago, the Carsons' trek on roller skates was a special challenge and a considerable achievement. Even though they were often traveling on the Lincoln Highway, most of that highway was not yet paved. Their specially made skates weighed four and a half pounds each and were riveted to their shoes. Once they put those clunkers on in the morning, they didn't take them off until retiring at night. Even though they often trudged over rough surfaces or through mud, they felt entitled to say they had skated all the way.

On May 31, 1921, the Carsons set out for San Francisco from Philadelphia, where Jack was a well-known exhibition skater and the operator of a rink. Although Blanche had not previously skated, she trained intensively for six months prior to departure and soon was an accomplished skater. Usually camping out each night, to cover their expenses they sold postcards as they went and gave skating exhibitions. Upon reaching Salt Lake City on July 10, 1922, they decided to go on to San Francisco by way of Seattle to avoid having to skate through a desert. They abandoned that plan at Pendleton, Oregon, in late September, however, and proceeded directly to Portland. Somewhere just short of that city, Blanche was overcome by exhaustion and hospitalized but, going on alone, Jack got to Portland in late May of 1923 and there ended the trek. Continuing to compete and perform, in 1926 the Carsons announced the opening of a rink "under the polite and decent management" of the "coast-to-coast roller skaters."

JACK and BLANCHE CARSON
PHILA. to FRISCO

Although Jack and Blanche Carson, shown here on their honeymoon postcard, were not the first to attempt to skate across the country, they were likely the first to succeed at doing so.

The Skate King

Sometimes a childhood enthusiasm may persist into adulthood and even become a determinative feature of a person's adult life. Roller skating played that part in the life of Asa Hall.

Hall got his first set of roller skates in 1897 at the age of nine, and by the time he was an adult, he was an expert skater. When not working at various odd jobs around his hometown of Mexico, Missouri, he could be found in rinks perfecting his skating skills or performing. Upon entry of the United States into World War I in 1917, he was drafted into the army, but he was discharged three months later because he suffered from flat feet. That was ironic, because in that same year he began to make heavy new demands on his feet. After reading about a man who skated from Chicago to Detroit, as he later told a reporter, he decided that "if he could do that, I could, too." Soon he had added longer ventures over rough roads to the skating he did on the smooth floors of rinks.

Hall's skating renown increased in 1929 when he skated on a $500 wager from Kansas City to New York in seventy-one days. As he gained recognition as the Skate King, he began planning a skating trek from San Francisco to New York. The Great Depression intervened, however, and Hall instead spent 1930 and 1931 skating throughout the Midwest looking for steady work. Finding none, in June of 1932 he skated off for Washington, D.C., to support the veterans rallying in pursuit of a bonus payment for their service during the war. Before he got there, however, both the Bonus Army and its lobbying campaign were no more. He resumed skating in search of work but, still finding none, in 1933 he removed his "I Am Looking for Work" sign and began skating for pleasure and the pursuit of knowledge about America and its citizens. For support, he would work when work was available and give exhibitions when that was possible, but most often he hoped to tap the largesse of people met on the way.

Hall's new approach, grounded in positive thinking and chutzpah, worked. Among his many later treks were ones to the West Coast in 1937 and to the New York World's Fair in 1939. By 1941, he claimed to have skated over 60,000 miles during his life and, as late as 1946, he was still adding more miles.

A photographer for Acme Newspictures took this shot of Asa Hall at an unidentified location on Hall's roller-skating trek from Kansas City to New York.

The Walking Fiddler

In what quickly became known as the Bunion Derby, 199 men departed from Los Angeles on March 4, 1928, in a footrace to New York City in pursuit of large cash prizes. Each day trucks carrying workers, tents, bedding, and food preceded the trekkers to set up at the evening's designated stop, where entertainers often performed. Fifty-five competitors survived the highly publicized race, which concluded in New York on May 26. As the gaudy show passed within several miles of his home in Hillsboro, Illinois, Otto Funk was inspired to concoct his own attention-getting cross-country trek that would take advantage of his prowess as a virtuoso violinist.

The sixty-year-old Funk owned and operated Funk's Lake, a recreational facility outside of Hillsboro, where he had also been a longtime music teacher. In 1915, one young violinist had already made the long walk from San Francisco to New York, earning income by performing as he went. For his trek, however, in addition to giving performances, Funk proposed to establish a unique record by fiddling every step of the way between New York and Los Angeles—that is, whenever he walked, he would fiddle, and when he ceased fiddling, he would stop walking. To sustain long periods of nonstop fiddle playing as the Walking Fiddler, he prepared a repertoire of 120 songs.

To be his advance agent, Funk recruited his son-in-law, Lester Grundy, who pulled a small trailer carrying bedding and supplies behind his Model T. Leaving New York on June 29, 1928, Funk mostly used U.S. 40 to St. Louis but there switched to U.S. 66. Encountering a blizzard in December, he hauled up in Amarillo for the winter. Upon resuming the trek in March, he extended his destination from Los Angeles to San Francisco, where he arrived on July 25, 1929, playing "California, Here I Come" on his violin. His trek had covered 4,165 music-laden miles.

Funk accomplished three goals on his trek—to earn money (or at least to cover costs), to advertise his music services, and to set a record. Thanks to Grundy's advance work, Funk gave many concerts, and according to *Guinness World Records* he stands alone for most miles walked while playing the violin.

The unidentified photographer of this Wikipedia photo caught Otto Funk
playing his violin for Navajo children somewhere in the Southwest in 1929.

Three from Texas

As the decade of the 1920s neared its end, America was treated to a final spurt of imaginative pedestrian treks. No sooner had Otto Funk's violin stroll ended in the summer of 1929 than three other treks of attention-grabbing novelty began (as also did a rerun of the Bunion Derby). All three were extraordinarily silly—a feature of many of that decade's enthusiasms—and all three came out of Texas.

Peanut Pusher

This photo of Bill Williams, accompanied by apt questioning of the significance of peanut pushing, appeared in the *Creston (IA) News Advertiser* on May 25, 1929.

Surely the most absurd trek ever undertaken was a brief but grueling mini-trek made in the spring of 1929 by Bill Williams, a forty-five-year-old plasterer residing in Rio Hondo, Texas. Losing a bet that Al Smith would win the 1928 presidential election, Williams had had to push a peanut with his nose over the eleven miles from Rio Hondo to Harlingen. Out of his friends' subsequent banter and guffaws came a new

A photographer for the *Houston Press* snapped this photo of Hoopie Williams rolling his hoop in Texas on his way to New York in 1929.

proposition—for a $500 purse, how about pushing a peanut by nose up the twenty-two miles to the summit of Pikes Peak within twenty-two days? Williams accepted and, donning felt knee pads and a nose extender, did the mini-trek with half a day to spare. Press coverage was enormous, but some of it did question the significance of Williams's achievement. On the other hand, a New York impresario reportedly offered him $1,000 to demonstrate his new skill in Madison Square Garden.

On July 6, 1929, two residents of Rule, Texas—G. C. Hart, a barber, and Luther Rose, a tailor—set out from Galveston to hit croquet balls all the way to New York City. Self-billed as the Crazy Croquet Cronies, they counted on getting funds by giving exhibitions as they went. When that didn't happen, folks back in Rule provided some support, but that was soon gone. After having dodged much menacing auto traffic for several hundred miles, they decided to end their bizarre trek in early August. Shortly before they did that, however, H. B. Williams, a twenty-five-year-old oil field worker from Texas City, accepted a wager to overtake and beat them to New York, all the while rolling a steel hoop with a fourteen-inch diameter and controlling it by dexterous use of a forked stick. Leaving Galveston on July 31, he stayed at it even after the Crazy Croquet Cronies pulled out, finally reaching New York on February 1, 1930. In recognition of his achievement, Williams became familiarly known thereafter as Hoopie.

Two More from Texas

The sudden rise of Texans to prominence in long-distance trekking in 1929 prompts some questions. What was it with Texas? Too, was there a family connection between H. B. Williams, the hoop roller, and Bill Williams, the peanut pusher from the lower Rio Grande Valley? And how to explain that from the lower Rio Grande Valley came two more zany treks during the next two years?

Ralph Sanders's postcard heralds his unprecedented ride on a bull from Texas to New York.

On their way from Texas to New York, Walter and Margaret Hofer paused in McAlester, Oklahoma, for this photo taken by an International Newsreel photographer on July 23, 1931.

The first of these new Texas treks was the production of Ralph Sanders, a twenty-eight-year-old cowboy residing in San Benito, Texas, who, as he told a reporter, decided that he "wanted to do something out of the ordinary." Concluding that no one had ever ridden a bull from Texas to New York City, Sanders bought a black bull, whom he named Jerry, and spent the next six months training. On May 14, 1930, they took off from Brownsville on an indirect route to New York, preceded by a truck carrying camping equipment and oats for Jerry and also by an automobile conveying Sanders's wife, their two children, and a helper. By that time, too, Sanders had been challenged to a race by a fellow townsman, who proposed to drive a goat and a donkey, start thirty days later, but still get to New York first.

Selling postcards as they traveled, Sanders and Jerry arrived in New York on January 20, 1931. They had covered 2,700 miles in 254 days, and their competitor had long since given up. However, Walter Hofer, a twenty-one-year-old truck driver from the lower Rio Grande Valley, was not impressed. Told that Sanders had done the trip in eight months, Hofer boasted to a friend that he could push his sister in a wheelbarrow over that same distance and still easily get to New York within seven months. That blowhard assertion couldn't pass without a challenge, of course, and, his sister Margaret agreeing to play her part, Hofer was soon entangled in a $1,000 wager to make the ridiculous excursion. Using a specially constructed wheelbarrow having a rubber-tired motorcycle wheel and a cushioned passenger seat, the brother and sister departed from Brownsville on May 28, 1931, aiming to be in New York by Christmas. By September, they had reached the Indiana border, having traveled 1,650 miles—nearly two-thirds of the journey. Regrettably, however, their newspaper trail ends there.

When Highways Were Stages

T HESE PAGES HAVE GIVEN BRIEF glimpses of nearly a hundred offbeat treks made or attempted across the United States (or substantial
portions of it) by about 150 trekkers of varying descriptions between
1867 and 1932. Although many more long-distance trekkers were afoot
during those years, those treated here offer a fair sampling of the wide
range of participants in this unusual activity. I confess to having gotten
immense enjoyment from excavating these accounts from the many
hundreds of articles I found in old newspapers. So bizarre and original
are some of these trekkers and their stories that of them it can truly be
said that "no writer could make this stuff up!" In addition to having
entertainment value, these accounts also provide evidence of vanished
features of an earlier American popular culture.

The latest treks that I treat in this book took place in the opening
years of the 1930s, which jibes nicely with the fact that the incidence
of cross-country trekking fell off abruptly in that decade and never
rebounded. By no means did it come to an end. Indeed, in 2013 an
investigator concluded that at any moment in recent years as many as
twenty long-distance trekkers might be on the road in the United States
(usually, it seems, engaged in promoting causes or pursuing goals of personal fulfillment or expression). No longer, however, do these latter-day
treks constitute a widely recognized category of popular activity, nor do
they attract the substantial participation and attention that they once
got. What dimmed the allure of cross-country treks after 1930 were the
Great Depression and World War II, as well as the steadily increasing
risks involved in walking along highways that carried ever more vehicles
moving at ever faster speeds. Not even back roads, increasingly hard-surfaced and filled with motorized traffic, could long provide exemption
from those dangers.

Harder to account for than trekking's abrupt decline after 1930 are its great vigor and vogue during the preceding four decades, especially the years from the opening of the twentieth century to the entry of the United States into World War I in 1917. Cross-country trekking's longevity certainly distinguished it from other well-known but relatively short-lived popular stunts, such as flagpole sitting, goldfish swallowing, and marathon dancing, yet it was no more financially rewarding, prestigious, or estimable than those fads.

Trekkers obviously secured enough wherewithal on their jaunts to keep going, but the usual return on the effort expended clearly was paltry. As for those big prizes and wagers for which trekkers claimed to be contending, in most instances they were fabrications. So, if not to secure money or other substantial material return, why did so many take up long-distance trekking? Not, it seems clear, because they could expect to bask in the hearty admiration of the public. Professional pedestrians in the nineteenth century were highly esteemed figures, but in most cases that admiration did not transfer to the cross-country trekkers who succeeded them in the next century. As my earlier pages revealed, newspaper accounts frequently derided trekkers as freeloaders, shirkers, and con artists, and trekkers' claims were usually greeted skeptically by the public. But why, then, did so many people turn out to greet them, listen to their spiels, buy their postcards, and often even give them free meals and lodging?

The answers to these questions, I suggest, lie by way of recalling an observation I made in the prologue and documented in subsequent pages, namely, that trekkers were performers and that America's highways, railways, and town squares provided stages for their arresting performances. Those stages were wide open for use by anyone having a yen to perform, and that so many did appear on those stages for many decades indicates that their performances connected with the tastes of the public during those years. Because the cultural fare available to most Americans at that time was so much more limited and locally generated than was so in later years, the arrival of a trekker from the outside world could summon excitement in a town and quickly give rise to a crowd ready to put skepticism aside and enjoy the show. Sometimes, as my earlier pages chronicled, a trekker might even be escorted into town by a marching band, engaged for a lecture or a performance in the local movie theater, or given a long write-up in the local newspaper.

That so many chose cross-country trekking as a field of performance, I would suggest, indicates a further feature of those opening years of the twentieth century in the United States. Historians have noted that those few years were unusual ones in American history, characterized as they were by widespread feelings of optimism and confidence but also by a complacency and an innocence that soon were abruptly shattered by the coming of war. Cross-country trekking clearly reflected these pronounced senses of self-assurance, ease, and personal empowerment. As frivolous, too, as it may have been, the enthusiasm with which it was done by so many for so many years also suggests that it may even have tapped into some of the same gusto that gave rise to the continent-spanning achievements celebrated at the Panama-Pacific International Exposition.

At the least, I conclude, the cross-country trekking phenomenon can be understood as a fitting tribute to those national achievements. Just ponder this fact: not many years before the heaviest incidence of cross-country walks, tens of thousands of settlers were still making their weary journeys west in ox-drawn wagons under conditions posing substantial risks and requiring dogged efforts. As these latter-day trekkers demonstrated, however, that same trip could now be done on foot in much greater safety, undertaken on a whim or carried out in comic style for reasons of personal display or amusement, and even financed in a banal manner by the sale of postcards to bemused spectators. Could there be a more dramatic demonstration of the successful completion of the American transcontinental project than that?

A Brief Bibliographic Essay

MY PRINCIPAL SOURCES FOR THIS BOOK WERE THE POSTCARDS AND photos distributed by the trekkers and the many hundreds of vintage newspaper articles that documented their trekking exploits. Absent the easy access to those articles made possible today by online newspaper archives, I could not have written this book. Another essential fount of information were the books written by the trekkers about their excursions. The titles and dates of most of those books, nearly all of them available today in inexpensive reprint or facsimile editions, I indicate at appropriate places throughout my book. To those entries should be added three more first-person accounts: Edward Payson Weston, *The Pedestrian's Adventures While on His Walk from Boston to Washington* . . . (available today as a facsimile copy of the original 1862 edition); Charles Lummis, *Letters from the Southwest* (Tucson: University of Arizona Press, 1989), a compilation made by James W. Byrkit of articles that Lummis wrote for the *Chillicothe Leader* as he trekked west to Los Angeles from 1884 to 1885; and Plennie L. Wingo, *Around the World Backwards* (Austin: Eakin Press, 1982).

In this book, I argue that the trekkers were engaged in a performance version of pedestrianism distinguishable from the more prestigious competitive pedestrianism and that Edward Payson Weston had much to do with the flourishing of both varieties of pedestrianism for many years after the conclusion of the Civil War. Three books that ably present the development and scope of competitive pedestrianism in nineteenth-century America are John Cumming, *Runners and Walkers: A Nineteenth Century Sports Chronicle* (Chicago: Regnery Gateway, 1981); Matthew Algeo, *Pedestrianism: When Watching People Walk Was America's Favorite Spectator Sport* (Chicago: Chicago Review Press, 2014); and Harry Hall, *The Pedestriennes: America's Forgotten Superstars* (Indianapolis: Dog Ear Publishing, 2014). Weston plays a featured part in both Cumming's and Algeo's accounts.

Providing more information about Weston is a good biography written by Nick Harris, Helen Harris, and Paul Marshall, *A Man in a Hurry: The Extraordinary Life and Times of Edward Payson Weston, the World's Greatest Walker* (London: DeCoubertin Books, 2012). Two books treat in depth Weston's transcontinental walk in 1909 at the age of seventy: Wayne Curtis, *The Last Great Walk: The True Story of a 1909 Walk from New York to San Francisco, and Why It Matters Today* (New York: Rodale Books, 2014), and Jim Reisler, *Walk of Ages: Edward Payson Weston's Extraordinary 1909 Trek across America* (Lincoln: University of Nebraska Press, 2015). Offering encyclopedic documentation of Weston's life and activities are two massive books by P. S. Marshall: *King of the Peds* (Bloomington, IN: AuthorHouse, 2008), 708 pages (!), and *"Weston, Weston, Rah-Rah-Rah!": The Original Sporting Superstar: A Career Biography* (Bloomington, IN: AuthorHouse, 2012), 723 pages (!!).

To the best of my knowledge, no previous book has addressed pedestrianism as a performance phenomenon. However, in the introductory pages of *Mavericks: A Gallery of Texas Characters* (Austin: University of Texas Press, 2008), Gene Fowler makes the case for understanding his zany subjects, some of whom were trekkers in the 1920s and 1930s, as practitioners of what later came to be known as performance art. Archibold Hanna, Jr., also hints at an understanding of trekking as performance in "The Genteel Explorers; or, When the Covered Wagon Became a Pullman Car," an article published in October of 1979 in the *Yale University Library Gazette*. There Hanna claims to have identified an unusual consequence of the development of a railroad network reaching to and throughout the West: "Once the comfort of rail travel had become the norm, the eccentrics and the nostalgics [such as the characters I treat in this book] reacted against it. Travel on foot, on horseback, or in covered wagon, no longer a necessity, became a challenge." That challenge soon took the form of many offbeat attempts at trekking across the country. Three of the four examples Hanna gives of "the eccentrics and the nostalgics" are trekkers whom I bill in this book as performance pedestrians.

A major sponsor of cross-country treks and many other eye-catching performance contests was the *National Police Gazette*, owned and edited by Richard K. Fox during the final two decades of the nineteenth century and the opening years of the twentieth century. An excellent account of Fox, his magazine, and his extravagant promotions is presented in

Guy Reel, *The "National Police Gazette" and the Making of the Modern American Man, 1879–1906* (New York: Palgrave Macmillan, 2006). For a generous sampling of the kinds of lurid articles, gimmicky competitions, and titillating illustrations offered in the magazine during Fox's years, see Gene Smith and Jayne Barry Smith, editors, *The Police Gazette* (New York: Simon and Schuster, 1972).

After attaining a modest level of notoriety via trekking, most of the figures treated in my book soon fell back into obscurity, where they remained until brought back to notice in these pages. However, accounts of at least some of these picturesque trekkers and their walking feats have reached print in recent decades. In several instances, the treks were episodes in lives sufficiently notable to have been covered in full biographies. In *American Character: The Curious Life of Charles Fletcher Lummis and the Rediscovery of the Southwest* (New York: Arcade Publishing, 2001), Mark Thompson provides a good summary of Lummis's trek. In an account of Ezra Meeker's life told in four volumes, Dennis M. Larsen devotes two of those volumes to Meeker's first trek on the Oregon Trail and to his continuing campaign to commemorate the historic trail; their titles are *The Missing Chapters: The Untold Story of Ezra Meeker's Old Oregon Trail Monument Expedition, January 1906 to July 1908* (Puyallup, WA: Ezra Meeker Historical Society, 2006) and *Saving the Oregon Trail: Ezra Meeker's Last Grand Quest* (Pullman: Washington State University Press, 2020). A much briefer treatment of Meeker's life and treks is found in Bert Webber and Margie Webber, *Ezra Meeker: Champion of the Oregon Trail* (Medford, OR: Webb Research Group, 1992).

Having spotted the dramatic, poignant, or humorous features of certain cross-country treks, writers have in four instances made those treks the subjects of entire books: Linda Lawrence Hunt, *Bold Spirit: Helga Estby's Forgotten Walk across Victorian America* (Moscow: University of Idaho Press, 2003); Charles B. Kastner, *Bunion Derby: The 1928 Footrace across America* (Albuquerque: University of New Mexico Press, 2007); Ben Montgomery, *The Man Who Walked Backward: An American Dreamer's Search for Meaning in the Great Depression* (New York: Little, Brown Spark, 2018); and Robert Hamilton, *The Lady Globetrotter: The Story of a Woman's Endurance* (Leipzig: Amazon Distribution, 2021). All four writers highlight the great human-interest potential of their subjects. Hunt's account of Helga Estby's trek is particularly moving and was indispensable to me in writing my brief account, as was Hamilton's book, which makes good use of the extensive correspondence sent by Lizzie Humphries during her desperate and doomed trek. Kastner provides a detailed and delightful account of the spectacular cross-country pedestrian competition of 1928, whose route happened to follow US 66, the newly designated automobile highway. Finally, Montgomery does an especially good job of embedding his account of Plennie Wingo's backward trek in its social, economic, political, and cultural contexts.

Other treks and trekkers have gotten brief coverage in book chapters. Some of the Texans whom I treat in chapter 5 received earlier notice in "Trek Stars: Hickey, Hoopie, Plennie L. Wingo, and Others," chapter 12 of Gene Fowler's *Mavericks*. In *Blaw, Hunter, Blaw Thy Horn: A Memoir* (Mahomet, IL: Mayhaven Publishing, 2011), Gary Forrester covers the violin-playing cross-country walk of his great-grandfather Otto Funk and reprints "The Walking Fiddler," an article written by Forrester's grandfather Lester Grundy that was first published in the *Modern Woodman* magazine in October of 1959. Brief accounts of the treks of Weston and Eli Smith, a U.S. mail carrier who traveled across the country by dog team, appear in Kenneth Wilson, *Snapshots and Short Notes: Images and Messages of Early Twentieth-Century Photo Postcards* (Denton: University of North Texas Press, 2020). And, although the fact is perplexing, "Walking around the World: From the Annals of Hyperpedestrianism" is chapter 14 in a book on medical anomalies by Jan Bondeson titled *The Lion Boy and Other Medical Curiosities* (Gloucestershire: Amberley, 2018). George Schilling gets five pages in a chapter that mostly addresses European trekkers and has no medical content.

Amid the clutter found on the internet are valuable resources bearing on the early trekkers and their odysseys. Well worth noting are articles written about long-distance walkers by Davy Crockett (yes, that is the name) and posted by him online at https://ultrarunninghistory.com. Crockett bases all his articles on very extensive retrievals of information from articles in vintage newspapers. Four of his accounts give ample coverage to trekkers considered more briefly in my pages: "Edward Payson Weston's 1909 Walk across America," "Dakota Bob—Transcontinental Walker," "Zoe Gayton—Woman Transcontinental Walker," and "The Wheelbarrow Man—Lyman Potter." Crockett also has posted articles addressing many attempts by Americans and Europeans to walk around the world. Among the trekkers he discusses in "Around the World on Foot—Part 3 (1894–1899)" are George Schilling and George Boynton. In "Walking Backwards around the World—Part 6," he treats not only Plennie Wingo but also Patrick Harmon and Jackson H. Corwin, even though neither of the latter two backward walkers aspired to walk beyond the confines of the North American continent.

Another substantial and useful article available on the internet is Susan Park, "The Life of Stephen Powers," a forty-five-page recounting of the very full life of one of the first persons to walk across the United States, arf028-003.pdf. Six much briefer articles also posted online that I found to be entertaining as well as informative are Brian Phillips, "Pedestrian Mania: How Edward Payson Weston Became the Most Well-Known Athlete in the World . . . in the 1870s," grantland. com/features/brian-phillips-edward-payson-weston; Greg Luther, "A Tramp across America: How a *Los Angeles Times* Editor Helped Create the Myth of the American West," about Charles Lummis, https://www. laphamsquarterly.org/roundtable/tramp-across-america; John Henry, "The Stranger Who Walked in—Literally—and Stumbled Out of Fort Worth's Hell's Half Acre," about Fred Miller, originally published in *Fort Worth* magazine, https://fwtx.com/news/features/tales-from-the-fort-the-stranger-who-walked-in-—-quite-liter; Richard J. Goodrich, "A Long Walk across America," about Ruth Harsley, Ethel Rockwell, and Maud Bridson, https://medium.com/history-of-yesterday/a-long-walk-across-america-c814006e1e8a; Melissa Davenport Berry, "The Legend of John Albert Krohn AKA Colonial Jack," americana-archives.com/post/the-legend-of-john-albert-krohn-aka-colonial-jack; and Cheryl Eichar Jett, "'Walking Fiddler' Otto Funk: Illinois Musician Walked across America to His Own Accompaniment," *Prairie Land Buzz*, April 2018, also at www.thebuzzmonthly.com. An article available at https:// patch.com>massachusetts>salem>mr-mrs-krom contains information about Mr. and Mrs. Harry Krom's later years as well as the Hartford fire chief's statement about their alleged 1917 house fire. Brief biographical accounts of some of the performance trekkers can be found online via Wikipedia.

The handful of long-forgotten bicyclists whom I cover in my pages all performed in the early twentieth century, and for information about them and their efforts, newspaper articles are the only source. However, some bicyclists not only made successful attempts to pedal across the country in the late nineteenth century, they also wrote accounts of their journeys. Those accounts are available today, and in recognition of the important place of bicyclists among the early trekkers, I list those writings here: Thomas Stevens, *Around the World on a Bicycle: From San Francisco to Tehran*, original edition published in two parts in 1887 and 1888, facsimile edition published by Read Books in 2013; George B. Thayer, *Pedal and Path—Across the Continent: A Wheel and A Foot*, original edition published in 1887, facsimile edition published by Echo Library in 2015; and George T. Loher, *The Wonderful Ride: Being the True Journal of Mr. George T. Loher Who in 1895 Cycled from Coast to Coast on His Yellow Fellow Wheel* (San Francisco: Harper and Row, 1978). Also, three excellent more recent books give close attention to the long-distance rides of three nineteenth-century bicyclists: Kevin J. Hayes, *An American Cycling Odyssey, 1887*, an account of a transcontinental bicycle ride by George Nellis (Lincoln: University of Nebraska Press, 2012), and *The Two-Wheeled World of George B. Thayer* (Lincoln: University of Nebraska Press, 2015), and Peter Zheutlin, *Around the World on Two Wheels: Annie Londonderry's Extraordinary Ride* (New York: Citadel Press, 2007).

Finally, to find evidence that cross-country trekking continues today, one need only go online to Amazon or eBay and enter "walking across America" or "biking across America" or variants of that heading. Doing so will quickly bring forth titles of many first-person accounts of recent treks across the country made on foot or by bicycle. For an anthology of brief accounts written by people who have walked across the United States in recent years, see Brian R. Stark et al., *Across America on Foot: 27 Stories of Adventure, Endurance, and Inspiration* (Bean Counter Crosser, 2020).